SWEATSHOPS IN PARADISE

SWEATSHOPS IN PARADISE

A True Story of Slavery in Modern America

VIRGINIA LYNN SUDBURY

iUniverse, Inc.
Bloomington

Sweatshops in Paradise
A True Story of Slavery in Modern America

turtle logo was designed and created by Robert Sudbury

iUniverse books may be ordered through booksellers or by contacting:

iUniverse
1663 Liberty Drive
Bloomington, IN 47403
www.iuniverse.com
1-800-Authors (1-800-288-4677)

ISBN: 978-1-4759-5377-0 (sc)
ISBN: 978-1-4759-5378-7 (e)
ISBN: 978-1-4759-5379-4 (dj)

Printed in the United States of America

iUniverse rev. date: 11/20/2012

For Dung and Nga, with great affection

Courage is not a man with a gun in his hand. It's knowing you're licked before you begin but you begin anyway and you see it through no matter what. You rarely win, but sometimes you do.

—Harper Lee, *To Kill a Mockingbird*

CONTENTS

PREFACE

I wrote *Sweatshops in Paradise* because you need to know this happened. I can write this story because I was the lead attorney for and friend to these garment factory workers. I lived and watched and argued these facts before the High Court of American Samoa. I did not write this story because I am exceptionally brilliant. When this case came to my law office, I was lucky enough to have bright legal lights illuminate the way.

Trafficking in people is a continuing, hateful, and enticingly lucrative endeavor. It occurs all over the world. It is alive in our fields and in our cities and possibly where we get a pedicure. It happened, in this story, in 2000 in an American territory. Make no mistake: slavery does not wear its cruelty on its face. It is oozing and convincing, and its price is right. It is not visible, as it once was. It is, nonetheless, the same abhorrent blight on our world.

You need to know this happened.

ACKNOWLEDGMENTS

Although I wrote this book, I am in no way solely responsible for the success of the lawsuit; I am merely the mouthy scribe. I would like to thank,

first and foremost, the Vietnamese and Chinese workers, who are the heroes;

Bill and Jane Hyman and the Concerned Citizen's Coalition, and Rob Stipp and the Seafarer's Center, for their very visible support and for teaching the workers English;

the *Samoa News* and most especially Lewis Wolman, for their coverage and his astute and insightful observations, which remain true after these many years;

Adeline and Dale Jones, for obvious reasons;

John Enright, and Katheen Kolhoff, for the quote "It's not the third world, but we can see it from here";

Michael Barcott, for pointing out that Tutuila was really "Chinatown, Jake," and for complimenting me for not turning white to black;

the Fund for Investigative Journalism, for their grant and for their belief in this book;

Stanley Togikawa, of the Southern Baptist

Convention in Hawaii, for being a tireless force in helping the workers when they got to Hawaii and placing them in homes throughout the United States;

Justice Lyle Richmond, for keeping his calm demeanor, integrity, and sense of humor throughout;

Joseph Grover Rees and Lan Dai Nguyen, for their intellectual insight and personal encouragement;

Heather Margaret and her family for their optimism and medical knowledge;

Maureen and Lionel Riley, for reminding me that the world was bigger than the island of Tutuila;

Melissa Barclay, for teaching me mahjong at a time I needed to be aware of clicking tiles and twittering birds;

Marty Duchnak, for reminding me of consistency and irreverence;

Susan Lynn French, Robert Moossy, and Lou deBaca, for righting a great wrong;

Petita To'aiti'iti, David Wagner, Jonathan Lane, and Mark Ude, for their efforts in preparing the workers for trial;

Barry Rose, Jennifer Joneson, and Steven Ford, for their thankless initial efforts for the workers;

David and Michelle Vargas, for teaching me how the legal world works;

Kathleen and Fisaga Kolhoff, for helping to start U'una'i and reminding me constantly of its worth, and for showing me what resolution and persistence look like in real life;

Catherine Buchanan, for believing in us and distracting me and making me laugh so hard I fell on the floor and realized I could be sane;

Scott and Alefa McPhee, for their humor, joyful attitudes, and constant evenness;

my dad, who told me to keep my head down;

my mom, who encouraged me to swim upstream;

Christa, who taught me a person could be unruffled and level throughout calamity;

my sister, Patty Ann, who lets me call her at three a.m. and never gets mad, reminds me that I am on the right path, is my constant cheerleader, and is the treasure of my heart;

and Rob, my breath and joy.

PROLOGUE

Rob and I left Mexican waters for the South Pacific in April 1995. We had been living and sailing in the Sea of Cortez, Baja, California, for the past six years. We sailed there from our home in Venice Beach, California, and lived aboard our sweet engineless sailboat *Scout*, a twenty-five-foot Pacific Seacraft. She was little but she was wiry.

We wanted to do a long ocean passage in *Scout*, so we decided to try the five-thousand-mile sail across the Pacific Ocean from Baja, Mexico, through French Polynesia and the Tuamotus, and on to the harbor of Pago Pago, on the island of Tutuila, American Samoa. We headed for Pago Pago because it was a territory of the United States and we could legally work. We had managed to keep the wolf from the door in Mexico by doing myriad activities, including boat deliveries and maintenance work, making rain sticks and beaded jewelry, writing, and running charters for the Moorings Bareboat Charter Company. We needed something new.

Scout was one of the strongest and best-built pocket cruisers in the world. Actually, at twenty-five feet she was probably too small to be considered a pocket cruiser; she was more a watch-pocket cruiser.

Rob and I had bought her in 1987 from a sailor named Peggy, and we realized early on that boats are live things that—like most live things—thrive on attention and care. Rob spent almost every day aboard and completely renovated *Scout*'s interior. He tore out her old dining table and used it to build the galley, which consisted of a one-burner brass propane stove, a teak drawer, a large brass bucket for the sink, and a brass hand pump for water. We bought new foam cushions and re-covered them in beautiful material.

We had only the one drawer aboard, so I spent lots of time pulling it in and out and deciding what would go inside. It slid well in Mexico but later swelled and got sticky in the tropics. I built a walnut spice rack (with close adult supervision). Robbie built a new dining table in butcher block with raised edges. He set scores of teeny rubies in the tabletop in the shape of the stars of the Northern Hemisphere in July so I would not forget them when we crossed the equator to the Southern Hemisphere. He hand carved beautiful teak latches for the closet and as holders for various tools. We had a Maxfield Parrish print framed in brass and put on the bulkhead wall—we had only a teeny bit of "wall" space and chose that print with great deliberation. The print is called *Stars* and is done in shades of blues and features a woman sitting on a rock next to the sea, gazing up at a starry sky. It evoked a sense of peace and wonder, and over the ten years we lived aboard *Scout*, we never tired of looking at it.

Scout flew dark tanbark sails and a black-and-red spinnaker when the winds weren't pounding. Her primary working sail was a huge tanbark genoa. Her hull was dark blue, and her shape was that of a North Sea fishing dory, pointed at both ends. Her tiller stretched out far over the point of her stern and attached to her enormous rudder, which curved gracefully along the lines of her stern, reaching into the water. A magic woman named Susan had painted her name on her stern quarters: "*Scout*" written with a hand pointing to her bow. Susan had also painted little smoke puffs coming from the exhaust port, since we had pulled her engine. On her bow *Scout* bore two eyes for seeing reefs and hidden dangers; Susan painted those below her waterline so she would see what Robbie and I couldn't.

Her beam was eight feet, and she drew three feet six inches fully loaded. She provided a far more comfortable ride at sea than many of the larger sailboats Robbie and I had delivered during our years in Mexico. She rode like a cork on the water.

The forepeak was spacious; we slept comfortably, even underway. Perhaps better underway—the sound of the ocean rushing past *Scout*'s hull and the tapping of the brine shrimp is a lulling music that I can still call up now. Being curled up in the leeward side of the forepeak was like being in a cradle. The only bad thing about sleeping underway was that one was inevitably sleeping alone; a cardinal rule aboard *Scout* was that a watch was always and without fail maintained while underway. The other rule was that while underway, we never, ever went out into the cockpit or up on deck without wearing our safety harness. I think these ranked right up there with "for better and for worse."

On late starry night watches, though, I would lean over *Scout*'s teak rails with my chin on her bulwarks, trail my fingers though the water as we sailed, and wonder what was down below all that blue-black wet. The great Pacific held layers of life and energy, and we were floating over that luminous universe. The water went down so far underneath us, it was impossible not to take some succor from the vastness and age and currently soft hold.

It sounds ridiculously manly to say that we sailed the Pacific because she was there, although in fact that is largely true. Perhaps that is why we undertake journeys—because they offer themselves up to us. We have no idea what they will hold or whether we'll succeed or even if we're really prepared—none at all.

Chapter One—Trouble Brewing

I believe it all started when Renee's dog committed suicide. It was in December 1999, around the first day of summer in Pago Pago, island of Tutuila, Territory of American Samoa.

The deceased, Midnight, had been an irritable big black dog with enormous teeth who was given to terrorizing passersby, me especially. Our law office was in an old house up the hill in the village of Fagatogo, and we had to pass Renee's house—and hence, Midnight—several times a day just to get to and from our office. I generally ran past that house at top speed; Rob just laughed and carried rocks. Finally, Renee decided something had to be done and secured Midnight to a stair railing with a long leash. One morning, rather than face a future that had him tied forever to the back steps, Midnight hurled himself off the top step and hanged himself. Renee's family, being a stalwart and realistic bunch, were not entirely undone. I later heard they got some kitties.

It probably wasn't the suicide, per se. It was like the winds changing, and the fact that once a girl sees a dead enemy dog hanging by its neck on her way to work, she knows that just about anything can happen.

"Virginia, can a woman get a divorce if her husband won't let her?" Grace, our secretary, wanted to know. Rob and I had just come into the office after walking up the hill and thinking of Midnight dangling from Renee's back steps. Her question got my mind off the death theme.

Our law office boasted a small (in number) but fiercely loyal Samoan staff. Grace, a mild, twenty-something mother with a soft New Zealand accent, was our secretary and receptionist and translator. She was the invaluable one who remembered faces and stories and helped me most. She tried to bring me coffee, but I dissuaded her with talk of feminist political correctness; when I brought *her* coffee, she was appalled. She wore the traditional *muumuu* or *puletasi* and had dark, curly hair. She had lived in New Zealand for her growing-up years. Many islanders had lived in New Zealand or Australia or had people there.

Our investigator was a kind, good-natured young Samoan man named Petita. He was taller than six feet two inches and weighed about 350 pounds. He had dark hair and a ready smile, and he would have walked through fire for Rob. He was one of the most loyal employees we'd ever known—not to mention one of the strongest. When we moved our office from Fagatogo to Nu'uuli, we rented the upstairs in a large building. We had to truck all the office equipment, books, files, and furniture up an outside full flight of stairs. I had just brought up something heavy, like a desk blotter, and had to stop to fan myself on the landing at the top of the stairs. Petita was hunched over below me, climbing the stairs. He carried a tall, four-drawer file cabinet on his back. The file cabinet was full. It weighed as much as a Volkswagen. He walked right up to the top of those stairs and set the file cabinet gently down next to me on the landing.

"Heavy," he said, grinning.

Our tiny office may not have been up to Baker & McKenzie standards, but it suited us just fine.

I walked into my office and looked at my Eleanor Roosevelt poster. She looked startled. I looked at my desk. It was covered with termite poo, or chewings, or whatever it is termites expel when they tear down a building in the tropics. By this time Rob and I had expanded the law office into half the upstairs space, so I was personally concerned with the fortitude of the building. Already there were weak areas in the floor, so when a large person—say, a Samoan—walked through the office, the floor heaved tremendously and made noises anticipating an immediate cave-in. (I could imagine the headline in the *Samoa News*: Client Falls through Second Floor, Needs Off-Island Therapy for Life; Lawyer Responsible.)

Grace buzzed. "Your eight o'clocks are here, Virginia." I looked at my calendar. This appointment was to be with a group of Vietnamese women who were brought from Vietnam to labor in the Daewoosa garment factory in the village of Tafuna. I believed they had a wage claim.

Grace escorted them into my office. There were nine of them. They were small women and looked even smaller to me then, as I was used to a larger local norm. They smiled shyly at me and held their hats and parasols in their hands. I had one lopsided black futon couch in my office, and they all sat on it. They all fit. They had dark, straight hair and extraordinarily bright eyes. They were a bit anxious but nonetheless looked at me directly. I felt an unspoken but palpable exchange of burdens.

Finally one of the women spoke. "I am Vu Thi Kim Dung. You know. I have some English." She pronounced her calling name "Zoong." She introduced the other women. I asked her where she and the other women lived.

"At Daewoosa compound, except for me."

"Where do you live?"

"At Ma and Pa Jones's."

"Where did you live before Daewoosa?"

"Vietnam."

"Where are your families?"

"Vietnam."

"How much are you paid by Daewoosa?"

"You know. No money; many months no money."

The meeting went on for some time. They became less anxious and more at ease and told me Daewoosa owed them wages for sewing. It was difficult for me to completely understand them, and for them to understand me, I'm sure. I wasn't unfamiliar with the difficulties of speaking a language different from my clients': I was a *palagi* (non-Samoan) in a Samoan world. Dung was still learning English but doing an admirable job at translating, especially at the times when there were ten people talking at once.

I got out several yellow pads, and we all drew pictures and handed them back and forth. The picture emerging was dismal. It appeared that the workers were owed money for back wages, and four of them had gone to see the Korean factory owner and operator, Kil-Soo Lee, the past April. They were thrown in the Tafuna Correctional Facility. The rest of the workers were told if they continued to push for their wages, they would be deported back to Vietnam. There would be a severe financial penalty—or worse—in store for them and their families.

"Why did you want to work in American Samoa in the first place?" I asked.

Dung translated this inquiry. The women exchanged glances, while several frowned at me. They conversed at length.

Finally, Dung answered. Her words echoed the sentiment held by immigrants throughout the years. It was a desire driven by ambition, a notion of freedom, and the hope of a better and more prosperous life. "It has the chances."

Grace buzzed me from the outer office, alarmed: Petita had discovered that a minion of the factory owner had covertly followed the workers to our office. Grace knew the man; he was a respondent in a particularly ugly domestic violence divorce case and was apparently doing a favor (or working) for Lee.

I told the women that I wasn't sure about taking the case. We walked into the outer office and set up another meeting for the next day at Adeline and Dale Jones's house in Pago Pago. The man who had followed them scooted into the office of the attorney with whom I shared space.

Dung tugged at my arm and pointed at him as he disappeared into the private office. "You know. That man, he is no good." She wagged a finger after him. "He follows us to your office. Mr. Lee is his friend."

One of the ladies clucked her tongue. "He is bad, bad for the workers."

"Ah," I said. "We'll see."

"Virginia," Dung stated. She turned and looked evenly into my eyes. "Will you help us?"

I hesitated. It looked like a simple wage claim to me, but there was that dead dog this morning. Something was afoot. Nine pairs of black and eager eyes now appraised me.

Dung touched my arm and smiled. "You know. You are the lawyer. You can help us," she said.

I turned and saw Grace looking at me, and Rob as well. Grace had her head turned entreatingly to one side. She seemed to echo Dung's words. Rob had that set look that roughly translates to "You can do anything you want if you try" or something equally and nauseatingly "cheerleaderish." I felt like Fred Gailey, that lawyer in *Miracle on 34th Street*, when Kris Kringle wanted help getting out of Bellevue. "I know you can get me out of here!" he told Fred. "I *believe* in you!"

The ladies were looking at me with trusting reliance. I had seen that same look on the faces of other clients. It meant that a load was now being shared, and shouldered, and some relief was being asked and some was being given. It made me feel older, and I wondered if this was supposed to make me wiser. I had been practicing law fewer than four years, and what I didn't know was astronomical.

"All right," I said, biting my lower lip. "Sure." The ladies nodded and filed out of the office, opening their parasols as they stepped into the bright Pago Pago sun.

American Samoa Congressman Ene [Faleomavaega Jr.] is concerned that BCTC [the local garment factory and forerunner to Daewoosa] is not doing enough to pave the way for local hires to take over from the Chinese sewers when their three-year permits expire in seventeen months. There is very little absenteeism amongst the Chinese, but the same cannot be said of the Samoan workers, who are very often absent. BCTC fired 261 local hires in a recent three-month period.

Re impending Daewoosa: Ene recalled the problems that Saipan has and stated he and Tauese definitely do not want American Samoa to become the home of an industry that relies on foreign workers.

—*Samoa News,* May 30, 1997

Rob and I decided to take the case pro bono. That really wasn't my intention at the outset. I was having a hard enough time billing for my services and kept taking things in trade when I knew clients couldn't really afford to pay cash for legal representation. (I got some swanky items in trade over the years: Samoan war clubs, chickens, breadfruit, and the like. Once I even got a wooden clock in the shape of a pineapple with a picture of downtown Waikiki Beach at night lacquered on the front.)

I knew that local attorneys Barry Rose and Jennifer Joneson, along with the US Department of Labor, had helped some of the Daewoosa workers earlier that year, and I spoke with them about the case. I realized there were some labor-related employment issues that I didn't normally encounter and could barely spell. Rob could handle the paralegal work for the case, but I knew I was in over my head and wanted cocounsel.

I called Christa Tzu-Hsiu Lin, a bright lawyer who had come to the territory two years before as a judicial law clerk for the High Court of American Samoa. Christa excelled in her prestigious position. She was Chinese American, spoke Mandarin, and was raised in Texas—a feisty and intellectual combination. Christa had ended her clerkship at the High Court and was now working as legislative counsel at the *Fono*, the American Samoa government (ASG) equivalent of the United States Congress. She was permitted by her employer to take private cases. She agreed to cocounsel the case.

Christa and I met with a number of the Daewoosa ladies and with a few Daewoosa gentlemen the next day. Many of the workers were present at the Jones's house, which was a beautiful two-story colonial overlooking Pago Pago Bay. Like most of the houses built on the island, louvered windows ran completely around the structure, which let in the almost-constant breeze off the water. Dale, in his sixties, was a former territorial liaison to the United States Secretary of Interior. Adeline, about the same age, was *afakasi*—half-*palagi* and half-Samoan. Her mother had been the premier *tapa* (bark cloth) maker on the island, and

Adeline had maintained the tradition. She was a tall, queen-like woman.

Christa, Adeline, Dale, Dung, and I sat at the main table, along with a worker named Ngyuen Thi Nga. Nga's mouth was shaped like a rosebud. She held a little sailor cap in both her hands and occasionally worried at it. The wind shifted and blew the fumes in from the tuna cannery across the bay. Adeline lit a menthol Benson & Hedges. I seized upon the excuse and whipped out a pack of Marlboros stashed in my purse. Rob and I had both quit smoking cigarettes, but only one of us actually stuck to it. I was forced to cop furtive puffs here and there, brush my teeth in my car, and eat heaps of Altoids. The wages of dishonesty are steep, but I did have nice breath.

"What do we know?" I asked.

"I've talked with Department of Interior," Dale said. "They're trying to work with immigration and to get Dung asylum status in the United States. She absolutely does *not* want to return to Vietnam."

"Is that possible?" Christa wanted to know.

"It's really difficult. There are a lot of channels to go through, and at the minimum she has to show a 'well-founded fear' of returning to her native country, Vietnam."

"Dung." Adeline poked her in the arm. "Are you afraid of going home?"

"You know." Dung narrowed her eyes and considered her folded hands. "I got a letter from my sister; she works at the Twelve Company. She says I might be in trouble, and maybe my mom also."

"Can we see the letter, Dung?" I asked. I hated prying into little crevices of intimacy in people's lives, but it seemed necessary to the case. "Do you have it?"

"Yes, downstairs." She went off to retrieve the letter.

"Adeline, what is that business about her mom being in trouble?" Christa asked.

Dale answered, "Dung's mother put up the original four thousand dollars for her recruitment fee so she could come and work for Daewoosa. She put up her house, and she's afraid she'll lose it if IMS thinks that Dung violated the contract."

"Can I see her contract?"

Dung returned and handed me the letter, along with several other papers. Among them was a document that looked like an employment contract.

"Do you have one of these also, Nga?" Christa asked.

"Yes. We all do." Nga produced her contract, and several of the other workers did as well. I collected the sheets of paper and handed them to Christa. "But *I* don't want to go to the United States; *I* want to go back to Vietnam."

Several of the workers nodded vigorously in agreement. One of the Daewoosa men workers had a question. "What if we get in trouble for the lawsuit?"

"What trouble?" I asked. "Trouble for what?"

Everyone now spoke rapidly, mostly in Vietnamese.

Dung waved her hands in the air, shushing the workers, and answered me. "You know, Virginia. In Vietnam we have a problem, we cannot bring the lawsuit. If we bring the lawsuit, we cannot work. We cannot say what is bad to the company or the government. It is the same here?"

Christa shook her head earnestly and answered. "No, Dung, it's not the same here. Anyone is allowed to bring a lawsuit and they don't get in trouble for doing so."

"They don't lose their jobs?" a woman named Thuy asked. She looked skeptical.

"Uh, no, not in theory," Christa replied.

Adeline snorted.

"But Dung has already lost her job! Mr. Lee told her not to work anymore," Nga reported, looking grave.

"She had a choice, Nga," Adeline replied. "Dung decided to come live here and leave Daewoosa compound."

"But she got put in the jail." Nga was undeterred. "Will we get put in the jail?"

This caused another uproar of rapid Vietnamese among the group.

"No!" I practically yelled. "Probably not I mean! This is *America*! We have a Constitution that protects us all!" I grabbed a yellow pad from my book bag and drew a picture of the United States. It looked more like a sponge, but I wrote "USA" on it and the workers all nodded in seeming understanding. My artist's depiction of the United States was fairly big on the page.

"And this! This is Vietnam!" I drew a teeny little speck over to the west. "Here, in Vietnam, something may be illegal. But here, in the big United States, we all have *rights*." I wrote RIGHTS in big letters. "Lots of rights! We can all think any way we like and express our opinions. We can hang out with anyone we want. If someone treats us badly, we can complain against him or her. And no one can make us work without giving us our wages. Do you understand?"

Thuy looked unconvinced. "But, in Vietnam ..." she began.

"This is not Vietnam! Look at the map!" I tapped it for emphasis. "Look how much *bigger* the United States is!" I was ranting and possibly losing the crowd. Dale chuckled.

I shot him a look. "Might does not make right!" I had recently reread *Idylls of the King* and was in a passion over the rule of law. "Right is right, and right will out. I'm sure of it." I was whining visibly now. "The United States doesn't condone this sort of behavior, and neither does the American Samoa government. *They* won't let this go on; we'll file the lawsuit and bring it to their attention and you—all of the workers—will be paid their wages. The ASG is not going to risk this much ill public sentiment over nonpayment of wages, and the court certainly will not allow such a thing to continue. Wait and see."

Later, Christa and Rob and I tried to piece together the workers' story based on the information they gave us. It was like starting a jigsaw puzzle without the final picture. (I figured it for a Gary Larson cartoon, the one that pictured a dingo farm next to a baby nursery with the caption "Trouble Brewing.")

CHAPTER TWO—JUSTICE IS
BLIND—GET OUT OF HER WAY

We still needed our day jobs. The year before, our law office had applied for and was awarded a grant from the Department of Justice's Violence against Women Granting Agency (VAWA) to open U'una'i Legal Services Corporation, the first free legal services, ever, in the territory. This focused us even more onto family law issues, but we also kept our small private practice in order to represent those clients who did not fall within the federal funding parameters. We named it *U'una'i*, which roughly translates to "self-sufficiency and empowerment."

I contacted our grant administrator at the Department of Justice in Washington, DC, specifically about U'una'i representing the workers, as they weren't victims of domestic violence or partner abuse so didn't strictly qualify for free services. I reckoned that I would ask, though, and had come up with a skewed but sincere analogous argument comparing the workers, who were subject to the whims of Kil-Soo Lee, to victims of domestic abuse. Washington was nice and compassionate and appreciated the novelty of the argument but still said no. We thus represented the workers under the auspices of my private law office, of which Washington both was aware and did not object. Our law office in Fagatogo was several steep blocks from the High Court. I generally walked down the mountain road to get to the court, often a few times a day. To get there I passed Renee's, then the Ripley's, and then Helga's Beauty Salon. That part of the village was shady with flowering plumeria trees. One day I passed a woman sitting under the trees. She was skinny by local standards and had wild and disheveled silver hair. She wasn't idle; she was pulling out the tiny plants that grew under the bases of the trees. She wasn't quiet, either: she yelled something at me about minding the falling leaves. Since there weren't any falling leaves this confused me.

A few nights after we and the workers met at Adeline and Dale's, I received an urgent call at home from Adeline. The ladies who had visited our law office earlier that week had indeed been followed by a minion of Kil-Soo Lee's. They had just been informed that they would be sent back to Vietnam that very evening; in fact, their sponsorships had already been terminated and deportation proceedings begun.

The American Samoa government has its own immigration office, which is not part of the US Immigration and Naturalization Service (INS). It is instead a fascinating manifestation of the façade of the INS: what the INS might look like if it moved to American Samoa but had only read one outdated guidebook. It made for a merry chase between illegal aliens, the capriciously zealous ASG immigration officers, the lawyers, and the courts. "Deportation proceedings" can mean a hearing, or it can mean that American Samoan immigration officers physically escort the alien to the ferry or to the airport. (Oftentimes this escorting is done without the voluntary agreement of the escorted.) The officers wait with the alien to ensure that the person leaves the territory. Although the American Samoa law does provide for access to extensive immigration hearings and review of any involuntary deportation, that procedure was routinely ignored.

Once the deportee is gone, she's gone, and generally no remedy exists without a plaintiff.

Rob and I picked up Christa and rushed to the airport. There, eight of the original nine ladies were preparing to board the first of many airplanes that would take them to Vietnam. They were happy to see us and hugged and thanked us over and over. Dung was wedged in between Adeline and Dale and was staying in American Samoa: she wanted no part of Vietnam. Rob waved us into camera range and told us to say "cheese." Everyone did and then started crying. Rob assured them that if we got their back wages, we would send it to them. We hugged again and watched them go. Several of them turned and waved as they went through the immigration check, and I knew I would never see them again.

Christa and I had to hustle to get the lawsuit filed and to forestall any more involuntary deportations of the workers. We drafted the complaint, and, with her permission, named Nga as our "lead" plaintiff. The case caption would thus be *Nguyen Thi Nga v. Daewoosa Samoa, et al.* She was nervous about the attention but was determined to obtain her wages. Several other workers were interested in joining the lawsuit, but since we had not yet positively identified them, we listed the plaintiffs as additional Jane Does. Others we named as defendants included Kil-Soo Lee, Lt. Gov. Togiola Tulafono, his wife, Mary, and the American Samoa government.

The sum total of what we knew at that point was this: Daewoosa Samoa, Ltd. was incorporated in 1994 in the territory and was funded by Kil-Soo Lee, who is Korean. Since he was not an American Samoan or a US citizen or national, he needed a sponsor to remain in the territory. We believed either the lieutenant governor or his wife or Daewoosa itself sponsored him. We could not find out then and still cannot to this day: the ASG will not release that information.

Lee opened the Daewoosa garment factory in late 1998, employing a score of Chinese men brought from China. In February 1999, forty Vietnamese women were brought to sew at Daewoosa by a Vietnamese government affiliated company named International Manpower Supply, or IMS. Daewoosa sponsored the Asian workers. The Vietnamese workers signed contracts with IMS that provided that each worker would earn $408 per month from Daewoosa, with the opportunity to earn up to $1000 per month in overtime. They would receive free room and board at the Daewoosa compound, and they would still receive their basic salary if the work was stopped by any reason not of their own fault or doing. There was a beautiful Olympic-sized swimming pool on the premises. Best of all, they would live in America.

In order to be eligible, however, the workers had to pony up between $4,000 and $7,000 per worker to IMS. This was a "recruiting" fee, and effectively indentured the worker to the company. Since the average daily salary in Vietnam was about one US dollar, the Vietnamese were understandably interested in this opportunity for financial gain. Houses were mortgaged at exorbitant rates. Money was borrowed from friends and relatives. The management contract included the clause that if a worker were to breach the contract in any way, she would be liable for a minimum of $5,000 US—to be paid to IMS.

In March 1999, forty Vietnamese workers had been sewing at Daewoosa for a month. They had not been paid their salaries. Toward the end of the month they each received $100 from Daewoosa. In April 1999 they still had not been paid their salaries as specified in the contracts.

To be clear: most of the garments that were sewn at Daewoosa Samoa arrived on the island in partially constructed pieces. For instance, the apparel was already mostly finished but still needed cuffs or hems or the like. There were some pieces of clothing that arrived completely constructed and all the workers did was sew "Made in America" labels inside them. We finally figured out that was why the location of American Samoa was so valuable to Kil-Soo Lee; it was America but it wasn't. Daewoosa got to proclaim that the garments were "Made in America" when in fact the attendant labor standards in American Samoa were so absent as to be a joke. Not to mention the lawsuit.

On April 15, 1999, the workers were eating lunch in the factory cafeteria. They were agitated and disturbed that they had not been paid their wages. The conversation level was louder than usual, and the subject discussed was the same at every table: how to get their wages.

Someone suggested they strike. This was not a new idea, although it was a radical one. There was a bit more discussion, and shortly a representative worker stood up at her table and cleared her throat. She addressed Chuyen, their Vietnamese overseer. She looked him directly in his eyes, defiant and intent. She announced that the workers refused to work until they received their wages. Angrily, Chuyen scurried from the cafeteria and headed in the direction of Lee's office.

Kil-Soo Lee stormed into the cafeteria, screamed at the workers in a combination of Korean and English, and violently overturned a table of food. He told them, through Chuyen, that if they went on strike they would not receive food. Several workers fainted. He ranted a bit longer and swept off toward his office, gesticulating wildly at Chuyen, who trotted alongside him.

Not ten minutes later a squad of large Samoan police officers marched into the noisy cafeteria. The workers watched, stunned, as the officers arrested four of the most vocal female workers, Dung included, and forcibly dragged them out of the cafeteria and into their squad cars. The women were imprisoned at the Territorial Correctional Facility for two days, unable to communicate with anyone at the prison. Lee had chosen the Vietnamese workers well: no one on the tiny island spoke Vietnamese well enough to communicate with them.

The workers left at the compound contacted Dale and Adeline, who in turn called Barry Rose. Barry and his law partner, Jennifer Joneson, were the brightest legal lights in the Territory of American Samoa. They, with the notable assistance of their associate Stephen Ford, got the ladies out of the prison and brought in the US Department of Labor, who investigated the situation at the factory.

By April, more workers were arriving from Vietnam to labor at the Daewoosa garment factory. By this time, however, most of them came through a Vietnamese government affiliated management company called Tourism Company 12, not IMS. TC12 supplied a total of two hundred workers to Daewoosa, all Vietnamese and mostly women. The workers signed the same contractual employment agreement with TC12 as the others had with IMS.

In May 1999, the Daewoosa factory was up and running. It was sewing and producing, thanks to the Vietnamese workers. Not all the Vietnamese were working, however; Dung and most of the original forty IMS workers were not. In May, Daewoosa terminated their sponsorship of the women who had refused to work. Dung alone wanted to go to the United States, and she thus had left the compound and moved in with Adeline and Dale.

Most of the remaining IMS workers were immediately deported; Daewoosa had terminated their sponsorship and informed the office of immigration. And because those workers had no sponsor, the American Samoa government immediately deported them back to Vietnam. In communications to the Vietnamese government, Daewoosa management further labeled those deportees as "troublemakers and agitators." In Vietnam, such a label can be a bad thing.

17

On December 29, 1999, Christa and I filed the complaint, alleging nonpayment of wages, breach of contract, tort claims, and Constitutional and due-process violations. We also filed a motion for injunctive relief, to prevent Daewoosa from arranging the deportation of more workers against their will. We pointed out to the court that Daewoosa had just had eight workers deported—illegally—because they had sought legal assistance. The High Court of American Samoa agreed, and Associate Justice Lyle L. Richmond granted our motion for injunctive relief and issued a stipulated preliminary injunction. This injunction prevented Daewoosa from removing or causing the removal of the plaintiffs (workers) from American Samoa or from otherwise fussing with them without talking to Christa and me. It was our first victory, of sorts, and it would have to carry us for a long time.

After filing the complaint, I walked back to our office and almost tripped over the silver-haired woman I had seen weeding a few days earlier. She still looked unkempt and disheveled. She told me the fruit was ripe. I thanked her. She seemed nicer than the last time I saw her. I never knew her name but called her Hertrudes in my mind (after St. Gertrude, the patron saint of cats, gardeners, persons with mental illness, and the recently dead).

COURT ISSUES TRO TO STOP DAEWOOSA DEPORTATIONS

Labor problems allegedly of its own making continue to

beset Daewoosa Samoa, Ltd., the beleaguered Tafuna-based clothing manufacturer.

The High Court issued a second temporary restraining order (TRO) against Daewoosa Samoa last Thursday morning preventing the company's management from harassing and or deporting any of its Vietnamese workers without court review and approval.

Defendants in the new lawsuit include Daewoosa Samoa president and chief operations officer Kil-Soo Lee and principals/incorporators Heung-Soo Jo, Moon Seung Kiyu, Yong Kyu Moon, Lt. Gov. Togiola Tulafono, his wife Maryann Tulafono, and the American Samoa government.

Filed by plaintiff Nguyen Thi Nga and at least thirty other workers listed as "Jane Does," the new complaint again addresses the issue of nonpayment of regular and overtime wages and also focuses on the US Department of Labor's wage settlement agreement that was reached earlier this year with Daewoosa Samoa.

The suit also alleges due process violations of local immigration laws, misrepresentation, breach of employment contracts, willful nonpayment of local taxes and FICA, withholding of passports and ID cards, false imprisonment, and harassment.

Local attorneys Virginia Lynn Sudbury and Christa Lin are representing the plaintiffs in their suit.

The TRO was signed by Associate Justice Lyle Richmond.

—*Samoa News,* December 28, 1999

Rob and I sold *Scout* in 1998, which had not been easy thing (but that is a story for another day). We moved into a little yellow house in the jungle on the side of a mountain. It had a tin roof, which meant you couldn't hear a person in the same room when it was raining. The building was falling down but it had a great porch that ran the length of the house and overlooked Fagatogo Bay. The house was teeny and had been built by Tuvaluvians. They tended toward compactness, which is perhaps why the ceilings were only seven feet high and not precisely plumb. The so-called living room measured nine by seven feet. Its size made it difficult to do certain yoga postures. We were the first tenants in the yellow house, but much of the wood had already rotted due to termites and wet. Living in American Samoa was like living in a Petri dish: warm and wet all the time. Rumor has it that there are numerous words for "mildew" in the Samoan language (and yet no word for "subtle").

Generally speaking, the walls in the yellow house didn't match up to the other walls, or the ceilings for that matter, which meant that animals the size of large rats freely came and went. We had coconut spiders the size of my hands, and geckos and skinks and lizards. There were rats that climbed the breezy coconut trees surrounding the house and vocal birds and fruit bats. Only the birds and bats did not come into the house. Our cats Janey and Zuzu lived in high cotton: the house and yard were rife with prey. (Over the years I must've peeled dozens of flayed gecko bodies off the bottom of my feet where I had stepped on them in the dark morning.)

The house itself was built on the edge of the mountain but still in the tropical jungle. The only way up to it, aside from hiking through the impossibly steep foliage, was the narrow cement driveway that angled up the side of the mountain. Its gradient reminded me of the streets in Pittsburgh. Unlike the streets in Pittsburgh, however, our driveway was edged by large, painted, fluorescent yellow-and-green polka dots that marked the edge of the cement and the beginning of the jungle growth. These nightmarish notations had been thoughtfully provided by our landlady's son, who had observed that his elderly mother, Rose, was having trouble identifying the edge of the driveway when she motored around the island in her blood-red Crown Victoria. These bright dots, presumably, would assist the old lady in not careening off the steep driveway, over the edge, and into the ocean below. As viewed from the main road, however, our driveway looked like it had perforations up its sides. Placement of these dots from hell was not limited to the edge of the driveway, either: they had been applied to the trunk of a palm tree that had fallen over the driveway and which stuck out a bit. (Better to paint the trunk fluorescent green than move the thing.) There was also a giddy fluorescent yellow bull's-eye painted on the side of a breadfruit tree in our yard, and some of our garden plants were shades not seen in nature.

Rob and I were home on the porch of the yellow house with our friend Marty celebrating the injunction in the Daewoosa case. It still felt like Christmas (as much as it can on a tropical island in the South Pacific) and we were looking forward to 2000. Who knew?

"Did you see the grave at Lolo's house?" Marty asked me. "It's something." We took wicked delight in the Christmas decorations on the island. Most houses were built on communal family land, and many of the residents' ancestors had been buried on that land. Their graves were often situated in the front yard and were marked by big stone or cement blocks the size of a small truck. They were built in layers, like wedding cakes, and were usually kept freshly painted and tended. At Christmastime, especially, they were the sites of great merriment. Festooned with sparkly tinsel and twinkly lights, in little swirly designs around the edges, they called cheery attention to the dead person interred below. Here's a grave! Party on me! Some of them looked so happy, like used cars lots in the night.

"What's at Lolo's house?" I asked.

"He's got a life-sized line of painted wooden reindeer pulling a sleigh that rides right up over the grave, which is decorated like a lighted airport runway ramp."

Rob laughed. "There's a crèche in Fogogogo that has Jesus, Mary, Joseph, and an inflatable Santa," he said. "And the Santa is wearing a Samoan-print ie lavalava (sarong) around his belly."

"How does the lavalava stay up?" I needed details.

"It's taped on."

"Ah."

"At least choir practice is over, though," I continued. "I couldn't get through to any government agency for months and I couldn't get much work done." Every year, the ASG orders its employees to take part in televised presentations of Christmas hymns, organized by agency. (The ASG owns the television stations.) Each agency purchases matching Samoan-fabric puletasis (tops and skirts from the same material) or muumuus or shirts. (The matching-outfit theme is of crucial import in American Samoa. I cannot exaggerate this point.) During the holiday season, ASG employees all get two hours every afternoon workday off for choir practice and oftentimes are so moved by the magnitude of the season and their musical contribution to it that they fail to return to work afterward. A large part of the American Samoa government is thus out of the office for a considerable period of time between Thanksgiving and Christmas. Every year, renegade employees, usually palagis, attempt to avoid these choir practices (and the resultant televised presentations). They encounter mixed reactions from the Samoans. Palagis are generally excused, due to our weird affection for the US Constitution and its heretical tenets of separation of church and state. Locals generally must attend.

"You expect too much," Rob noted. "You think you can come to Tutuila and expect things will be as they are other places you've lived. Three thousand years of Samoan custom on one side and you on the other."

"Whatever." I was vexed. "People should do their jobs, is all."

"They do. They just do them differently than you," Rob pointed out.

We pondered that notion in silence and enjoyed the spectacular view. A big rat scampered across the side yard, headed for a coconut tree. Rob reached over and grabbed his wrist slingshot, which was always kept handy to protect us from dangerous and unwanted visitors, like stray kitties. He quickly loaded a marble in the sling and fired it at the rat. The rat was knocked clean over onto its back and was still, its four legs straight up in the air. It looked like a cartoon. We were all amazed at this masterful display of marksmanship, Rob not the least. It was a good day in paradise.

US DEPARTMENT OF LABOR GOING AFTER DAEWOOSA, AGAIN

Daewoosa Samoa's legal problems have grown by leaps and bounds now that the US Department of Labor (DOL) has accused the company and its officers of numerous, serious violations of the federal Fair Labor Standards Act.

The DOL's petition follows almost three weeks to the day a similar filing by local attorney Virginia Sudbury on behalf of several Daewoosa workers whose primary complaint was nonpayment of wages, both regular and overtime.

Sudbury also sought an injunction to prevent Daewoosa Samoa from hurriedly returning its Vietnamese workers back to their homeland without the due process of immigration law. The injunction was granted by the High Court.

—*Samoa News,* January 12, 2000

Chapter Three—A Very Curious Girl

When I was hired by the ASG public defender's office in 1996, I had never really practiced law. I had graduated from law school in 1982 but decided that I really didn't care much for lawyers or being one. While I knew the law, I didn't know the practice. Fortunately for me, Rob and I recently acquired a television (the first in seven years) and we watched a lot of courtroom dramas, which I intended to imitate to the best of my ability. (Fortunately for the High Court of American Samoa, we had moved beyond Perry Mason.) I read the American Samoa Code Annotated and the Administrative Code and the court rules. I went to the law library. I had an excellent teacher in David Vargas, the first assistant public defender. David is a smart-mouthed experienced attorney who is sharp as a whip and does not suffer fools in the least. With me, he suffered a *lot*. He was remarkably patient, though, and always available to answer my million questions.

The office of the public defender was located in the Executive Office Building in the village of Utulei. Utulei was one village over from the village of Fagatogo, which housed the courts. Flo, the receptionist at the public defender's office, was a twenty-something Samoan woman, married, with children. She could answer the telephone and pronounce "Public Defender's Office" in two syllables. Such facility fascinated me. The office seemed really up-to-date: it had one computer. I knew next to nothing about computers and was excited with the prospect of learning about them. It was difficult to learn much, though, as Flo used it to play solitaire and tended toward snippiness when I asked her to stop and prepare a pleading for me. I ended up doing my own pleadings, which is what I learned the other government lawyers did.

I left the public defender's office in early 1997, and Rob and I opened the private law office. We had a general civil practice, which meant we handled everything from admiralty law to criminal defense to trespass-by-falling-leaves to music copyright lawsuits. Mostly, though, we did family law.

Family law was a thing in and of itself on the island of Tutuila. Most of our family law clients were women who sought a divorce from their husbands. They came to us surreptitiously, and almost all asked us the same initial question: Could they get a divorce *without* the consent of their husbands? They had been told they could not. They marveled at the truth and still some left unconvinced, shaking their heads. The other thing they had in common was the fact that they had almost all been beaten by their husbands. They had been raised to believe that women were unequivocally inferior to men. In many ways, their situations paralleled that of the Daewoosa workers.

By January 2000 both Rob and I had learned how to research legal issues, file court pleadings, operate a computer, and run a law office. U'una'i was successfully rocking along in its little falling-down office and had more clients every day. Christa or Rob or I communicated with the Daewoosa workers on a daily basis. We met at Adeline and Dale's house, or at the office late, or out at the Daewoosa compound; or talked, through Dung, on the telephone.

More Vietnamese workers quietly came to our office during the day and haltingly called us at night to ask if they might join the lawsuit (which was now accelerating toward class-action status). A class action is a specific type of lawsuit. To be accorded class-action status from the court involves some procedural hoop-jumping. At its most basic, there had to exist common elements of fact and parties: several people had to be harmed in approximately the same fashion or as a result of the same bad antics of the defendant. We had plenty of necessary plaintiffs. There was no strict minimum number of plaintiffs for a class-action lawsuit (at least there wasn't in 1982 when I graduated law school). We had plenty: more than 150 workers had then told us they wanted to join the lawsuit. Christa and I began doing research at night; she discovered there had never been a class-action judgment issued in the territory.

On January 26, 2000, we filed a seven-count motion for injunctive relief against defendants Daewoosa and Lee. We alleged they not only weren't paying our clients, they were bringing in more workers to the territory from Vietnam and continuing their threats to deport the resident workers. This course of conduct amounted to an illegal mechanism of resolving labor disputes and was in direct violation of the December 1999 injunction. We also alleged that the workers were not receiving nutritionally sufficient food, access to medical care, and the defendants were illegally retaining the workers' passports and ID cards. We asked that the court enjoin Lee from leaving the territory. We knew this last request was soft constitutionally but we were starting to fret about his leaving American Samoa. And besides—you don't ask, you don't get.

Our motion was set to be heard on January 31, 2000. At that time an attorney named Malaetasi Togafau was representing Daewoosa. Malaetasi was a former ASG attorney general; after his term ended he went into private practice. He had recently been elected to the *Fono*, the American Samoan congressional body.

The *Fono* is the American Samoan equivalent of our US Congress. It is comprised of the House of Representatives and the Senate. Most of the lawmakers are men. The representatives are elected in approximately the same fashion as they are in the United States. The Senate, however, is made up of *matais*, high chiefs. Only chiefs are allowed in the Senate. When in session, the legislators are flanked by two American Samoan gentlemen dressed in traditional garb: *ie lavalava, ula* (seed necklace) around their necks, holding *to'oto'os* (tall and imposing "talking sticks").

The High Court building in downtown Fagatogo is the former United States Navy administration building, built in the early part of the 1900s. The early (and intense) navy presence on the island has since moved on to drier pastures and the impressive structure was appropriated as the courthouse. Made of white clapboard, wide verandas circle it almost completely on both stories—bringing to mind a courthouse in the Deep South of the United States. It had big green and white double doors that opened onto the wide veranda downstairs, a place where clients, police, families, and attorneys gather. The veranda was a great spot to talk and smoke and try to convince the other side that their case was a loser, and if you stood there long enough (say, a few seconds) you would certainly see someone you knew drive by, honk, and wave.

The building housed two courtrooms: one upstairs and one downstairs. The larger, downstairs courtroom is the official province of the chief justice, Michael Kruse. That courtroom has twenty-foot ceilings, its walls are dark varnished paneled wood, and it carries an aura of salt and stoicism and wavy tropical heat. Banks of windows provide a view onto the encircling veranda and the ubiquitous churches beyond. The three judges—the chief justice flanked by two associate judges—sit in typical raised-bench fashion. The courtroom is imposing when empty but commanding when the chief justice is on the bench.

Chief Justice Kruse generally terrified me. He is half Samoan and half German and about six feet two inches in height. Clearly I am not one given to exaggeration, but when Chief Justice Kruse was on the bench he seemed twenty feet tall. On one occasion I saw him send his bailiff out into the hallway outside the courtroom to yell at the people in the hall for being too noisy. Once, during a trial, he told me that he was going to hold me in contempt and toss me into jail if I didn't wipe the "defiant" look off my face. I instantly cultivated a "respectful, yet not totally convinced" look on my face. Chief Justice Kruse unquestionably ruled the High Court, in both demeanor and appointment.

Associate Justice Lyle L. Richmond's courtroom was upstairs. You got there by climbing the wide carpeted stairway, which opened onto the upper landing. It was smaller than the first-floor courtroom but had full windows and a door opening onto the second story veranda. The raised judge's bench sat facing the courtroom with its back to the windows, which overlook Pago Pago Bay and the tuna canneries. The right counsel table sat next to the bookcases. The left counsel table, though, had a bird's-eye view of the hopping Fagatogo marketplace and part of the main road. This stimulating vista could add thrills to even the most tiresome hearing, and I usually charged past the bar to get to that table before opposing counsel did. (Once, during a trial, I was walking about the courtroom, examining a witness, and I looked out the window and saw my friend Kathleen drive by. I almost waved but stopped myself in time.) The upstairs courtroom had a more intimate feel that the downstairs one lacked. Perhaps it was the "kinder, gentler" courtroom.

When I pulled into the parking lot of the High Court for the January 31, 2000, hearing, it was raining heavily. I pulled my purple flowered book bag full of court files out of the car and ran to the covered courthouse veranda. As I sprinted up the wooden steps, I saw Hertrudes. She was hunched next to the courthouse. She was wearing a black trash bag with holes cut out for her head and arms. She glared at me and pointed angrily at the wet dank sky. *Pea lava pea.* Now and always.

On January 31 the upstairs courtroom was packed with our Daewoosa clients and their friends and supporters. Bill Hyman, who taught Dung English was there, as were Adeline and Dale, Fili Sagapolutele and Richard Coleman from the *Samoa News*, and members of the Concerned Citizen's Coalition, a group of locals concerned with the workers' plight. And so many of our clients came—more than eighty or so were present—at the first public event at which they could actually be physically identified by their oppressor Lee.

The workers and we had all engaged in much advance discussion about their presence at the hearing, and how such a visible action might affect their jobs. They seemed acutely aware of the trouble Dung and the other outspoken workers had experienced, and, although concerned, were resolute. They squeezed into the courtroom benches and whispered among themselves. They carried umbrellas and wore hats against the sun, and some had little spiral notebooks and pens. All of them hugged us and shook our hands and thanked us over and over. If we had a penny for every time a worker thanked us during that lawsuit, Christa and Robbie and I would be as financially wealthy as we are emotionally changed.

We both felt strongly that the workers be involved in every hearing and every decision and should derive some empowerment from the action itself. At the January 2000 hearing, we received the translating assistance of Nya, a Vietnamese attorney on the island for a short time. Our clients knew what was happening every step of the way.

On the day of the hearing, Christa and I secured the preferred panoramic counsel table early on. Mr. Lee came in and sat at the defense table. He wore a beige silk suit and flashy two-toned beige-and-white shoes. His socks matched the outfit and each other. He was smirking, an indelible expression that would become his trademark and one that Christa and I would learn over time to truly despise. He bowed and tried to shake hands with Christa and me but was rebuffed, probably rudely, by me. I am aware that there is merit to being polite to those we dislike, or even hate, and that is definitely the high road that should be taken by gentlewomen everywhere. Sometimes, though, it is just purely impossible to smile at a bad man.

Mr. Lee had an entourage who had come to court to support him, including a man we called Small Lee, some Samoan workers, and Lee's interpreter, Il Sang Lee. Il Sang, from what I had been told, was of certain stature in the Korean community in Pago Pago and seemed peevish about his role in this dirty mess. He appeared to want to be anywhere else.

Also in the Lee Band of Minions was Virginia Solia'i, the secretary to Lee at the factory. She was also a *de facto* liaison between Lee and the thirty or so Samoan workers, and she relished that powerful role. (It still frosts the heck out of me that she and I share the same calling name and initials.) The other members of the ensemble were Robert Atimalala, a top Daewoosa manager/liaison, and Elekana Nu'uuli Ioane, the Samoan floor manager. Nu'uuli was called a *fa'afafine*. In the Samoan language, *fa'a* means "in the way of" and *fafine* means "girl."

Ms. Temukisa, the clerk, ordered us to stand, and Justice Richmond, Associate Judge Autilagi, and Associate Judge Tauanu'u filed in. Justice Richmond sat in the middle and was flanked by the associate judges. The court heard our appearances and disposed of a legalistic matter: the dismissal of the additional named defendants. We wanted two kept in: Togiola Tulafono and his wife, Mary Tulafono. Togiola was the lieutenant governor of America Samoa. He was Lee's first on-island attorney and had allegedly advised Lee extensively on Daewoosa's local set-up and incorporation. He also held, within the ASG, the curious role as procurer of foreign investment in the territory. His wife, Mary, sat on the board of Daewoosa in the role of secretary.

During the proceeding, their attorney, Roy Hall, moved for their dismissal as defendants and alleged no participation by the Tulafonos in the affairs or activities of Daewoosa. He prevailed, and the Tulafonos were out of the loop, at least for the time being.

We then moved to amend the complaint to add both defendants and counts. The court granted that motion, and next heard our motion to certify the named workers as a class. Christa and I had researched the thing (although we still had miles to go) and had written a good supportive memo.

The court asked Malaetasi what his position was on our motion. Malaetasi replied, "In the first place, Your Honor, I did not have the opportunity to review that motion because I just returned back on Friday night. I was off-island for a funeral. And I just got back on Friday night. I'm not quite sure why she wants to file this as a class action, but she's able to identify the individuals who were involved in this case. Now she's filing a second motion, which I did not have the opportunity to review yet, to look at it saying it's a class action." He struck a righteously indignant pose. In response, the court announced that it needed to study the class action status first and reserve its decision.

Justice Richmond wanted to hear the testimony on the show cause re contempt request we had made, and our motion for injunctive relief. When the court issues an order (or prohibition, such as one forbidding certain behavior) and the party against whom the order was issued violates it, the wronged party can file an application for an order to show cause re contempt. Then the offending party gets hauled in before the court, and a variety of remedies can happen. He can get slapped on the wrist and told to go and violate no more. He can get fined. He can even get thrown in the jail. The court has an extraordinarily wide-ranging choice of options.

The subjects of the show cause hearing that day were our allegations that Lee and Daewoosa were threatening our clients with termination of their sponsorship (which would result in their deportation by ASG immigration) without the opportunity for proper consultation or hearing. We also alleged that Lee and Daewoosa were disturbing the workers by retaining Nga's alien ID card. In the territory, aliens (non-American Samoans or non-US citizens) had to carry their alien ID card with them at all times. Failure to do so was a misdemeanor.

We called Nga to the stand. She was poised but a little bit nervous, especially with Lee and his cronies smirking at her.

Christa conducted foundational questioning of Nga. "Where do you work?" she asked her.

"I work at the compound in Daewoosa."

"Where do you sleep?"

"I live at the compound in Daewoosa, at the female section."

"Can you describe your meals?"

"Rice, potatoes—sorry. The meal is rice and potatoes, rice and some noodles and sometimes with some chicken."

"Where is your passport?"

"Since I got here, I do not know where my passport is."

"Do you know who has your passport?"

"No. I don't know where that is."

"Did you give your passport to anyone?"

"I arrived at the airport, and I gave it to Mr. Lee."

"And what about your ASG alien ID card?"

Nga looked directly at us when she answered. She looked taller. "On January 14, I lost the card. I went to the entrance and gave the card to the security guard, and when I came back, I didn't know where it was. Neither did the security guard."

"Has your ID card been replaced?"

"No. I don't have a new one at all."

"Why not?"

"I went to report it to Mr. Lee, and I asked him about it, and he said we'll wait until the hearing, and we'll sort it from there."

"Nothing further," said Christa.

Malaetasi cross-examined Nga. He placed his hands flat on the counsel table in front of him and leaned into the table, looking intently at Nga. "Isn't it true that you lost your own ID card?"

Nga met his eyes. "I go to the gate, and if I don't give my card, then I won't be able to be let out." Nga's testimony concluded on a stalwart note and she was excused from the witness stand.

Next we presented testimony in support of our allegations of deportation threats made by Lee against the workers. We called Phuong Nguyen, who testified that she was told to attend a meeting on January 15 in the Daewoosa office. Four other workers were also ordered to attend that meeting. Present also were a Korean Daewoosa manager named Mr. Sung, and Kil-Soo Lee himself.

"What, if anything, did Mr. Sung tell you?" Christa asked.

"He asked why we were not going to work. After he asked why we weren't working, I said we hadn't been paid. That's why we weren't working."

"Did Mr. Sung say anything else?"

"Mr. Sung said if we don't go back to work today, that we'll be deported to Vietnam."

"Did he say when?"

"On that day it was Saturday but he said that we would be deported on Friday next week."

"Nothing further."

Malaetasi made the point on cross-examination that it was Mr. Sung who had made the deportation statement and not Lee. We moved on to our next witness, Duong Thi Minh Tam. Tam was in her midtwenties, possessed an inherently cheery nature, and generally looked like she was on the verge of bursting out laughing. Her eyes almost always sparkled and she was one of those persons who made you feel better just being around them. I got through the necessary foundation and asked her about the food at Daewoosa.

"Does Daewoosa supply all your meals?"

"Yes, they do."

"Can you describe the meals, please, for the judges?"

"Okay. We eat rice three times a day. The meals consist of rice and potatoes and rice and some noodles and sometimes rice and some chicken."

"Do you always get chicken?"

"No."

"Are there some days that you only get rice or rice soup?" I was leading her blatantly but Malaetasi either didn't notice or didn't care.

"Usually, every Sunday morning, we just have rice soup. And there are some people who are unable to just eat rice soup and so they have to go and buy their own food."

"Why do the workers need to do that?"

Tam nodded and answered. "Okay. There's not enough nutrients. They have to go and buy extra food so that they can physically do the work, just to do the work at Daewoosa."

"Have you ever seen anybody faint as a result of the food?"

"Yes." There was a tittering agreement from the workers in the courtroom. I had nothing further. We presented a few more corroborating witnesses and rested.

Beginning his case-in-chief, Malaetasi called a Vietnamese woman who worked in the Daewoosa office, a Ms. Haung, to counter Tam's nutritionally deficient food testimony. She chose not to testify in Vietnamese and instead spoke in poor English. She looked resolute and nodded to Malaetasi before he began his direct examination. He went through the foundation describing her job in the office before asking about the food.

"Do you eat in the cafeteria of Daewoosa Samoa?"

"Yes." Ms. Huang glanced nervously back to the workers in the courtroom, who were listening attentively to her every word. "Three meals a day." There was a rustle in the crowd.

"Three meals?"

"Yes."

"And that's from Monday to Sunday?"

"To Sunday, yes."

"Every week?"

"Yes."

"Could you describe the type of meals or type of food that has been served there?"

"It's—I don't remember exactly, but I think is a lot of kind and enough for my health and my work at Daewoosa." I looked at Christa and rolled my eyes. Ever the professional. Behind us, there was a louder tittering, definitely hostile.

It was then our turn to cross-examine Ms. Huang. "Can you tell me what your job at Daewoosa actually is, please?"

"My job is I work in the—I'm staff in the office. And I make the document in the Daewoosa. I make the document and I check the time, working time of worker in Daewoosa."

"So you work in the office?"

"Yes."

"And you work with management, correct?"

"Correct."

"Are you a seamstress? Do you sew with the workers?"

"No. I'm not sewing."

"You strictly stay with management?"

"I work with management, but I live together with workers."

"Do you know what your earnings are compared to what the workers earn?"

"Yes."

"Do you make more than the workers?"

"Yes."

"How much more?"

"It's up to the—up to the time of working of worker because a worker ..."

I was confused and sure that she was being purposely evasive. "Ms. Huang, do you prepare the timesheets?"

"Yes."

"And approximately how much more than the workers do you make per month?"

"I cannot be exactly."

"Ms. Huang, how much do you earn every month at Daewoosa?" The workers in the courtroom were quiet as mice.

Ms. Huang looked beseechingly at Justice Richmond. "I think if I must answer this question?"

Justice Richmond nodded at her. "Yes, you must answer," he stated.

Ms. Huang hesitated just a moment. "It's nine hundred." The workers behind us gasped.

"Nine hundred every month?" I asked.

"Yes."

"Is that before or after deductions?"

"After."

"How much do you make *before* deductions, Ms. Huang?" She looked confused and shook her head. I tried again.

"Ms. Huang, you are in charge of preparing the books and the payroll?"

"Yes, but my salary is a management pay from me."

"How much do you make per month?"

"Is nine hundred."

"*Before* deductions?"

"I don't know. I just receive after deduct."

"You don't know what your salary is before deductions, is that your testimony?"

"Yes."

"And *you're* the person charged with keeping this paperwork for the Daewoosa Corporation, is that correct?"

Ms. Huang nodded. She looked less resolute now.

We made our closing arguments and called it good. Lee and Malaetasi left the courtroom, surrounded by the minions. Lee was smirking. I glared at him. The smirk remained.

Nineteen days later we received the court's decision on the issues raised at that hearing. Justice Richmond had granted our motions to add both counts and defendants. On the show cause request, he stated that "... Daewoosa and Lee are guilty of willfully and contemptuously violating the [earlier] injunction by threatening and intimidating the employees." He also noted that Daewoosa was no longer entitled to hold our clients' ASG alien ID cards and found that "there is a substantial likelihood that plaintiffs will succeed in showing that Daewoosa provides inadequate food for its employees, and we can think of few instances that would constitute a stronger showing of irreparable harm improper nutrition." Although hesitant to set forth a particular diet, he cited to USDA dietary guidelines for Americans and provided the website.

Ultimately, he held Daewoosa and Lee in civil contempt and fined them each $5,000. They paid almost immediately. Ten thousand dollars was nothing to them, we saw.

Chapter Four—It's Not the Third World, but We Can See It from Here

By February 2000 Christa, Rob, and I were fielding all manner of questions from our clients. They were feeling comfortable with us, and we conversed and met more often. We discovered that the Daewoosa compound had been without electricity for an entire weekend, since Lee had failed to pay his electricity bills. The *Samoa News* reported this and noted also that someone had called the paper to report that the Vietnamese workers were sitting, en masse, a few blocks down the street from the Daewoosa compound. They were sitting on the ground, crowded into a large semicircle, eating their food with the help of a light cast by a nearby streetlight.

The US Department of Labor also came back into the picture. This time, however, they pulled no punches. They accused Lee and his alter-ego Daewoosa of serious violations of the federal Fair Labor Standards Act. Apparently, when DOL representatives had visited the Daewoosa compound in May 1999, they had taken offense at the way Daewoosa was doing business. Specifically, they charged that Daewoosa repeatedly violated the FLSA by paying the workers less than the applicable statutory minimum wage, taking kickbacks, confining workers to their quarters, not paying workers' wages, not keeping adequate records of employees, and so forth. DOL had also brought their consent judgment before the High Court of American Samoa. That consent judgment was signed in August 1999, and in it Lee admitted violating the FLSA and promised to never do it again. Christa and I were pleased; we felt that the US Department of Labor was a mighty force and that having the consent judgment in the picture could only strengthen our case. In the meantime, local awareness of the case grew.

DEAR JUST ASKING

"I thought *Samoa News* quoted the governor as saying something like, 'If Daewoosa breaks local laws again, I won't hesitate to throw them out.' Now they have admitted to not paying employees as well as many other illegal activities; was the governor just talking to himself? I'm just asking ..."

We put your question to Governor Tauese Sunia Monday. He said he stands by his earlier words, but he also said that the recent court decision involving Daewoosa stemmed from the original complaints against the company, not a new series of proven allegations.

He said if a new crop of violations were proven, he would be prepared to take action because American Samoa cannot afford to gain a reputation such as Saipan, Northern Marianas, has.

"Daewoosa is not like Saipan, where the employees are housed in stacked bunks and transported to work standing on the back of a truck, as if they were soldiers," Tauese said. The governor also said it is up to Lt. Gov. Togiola Tulafono, who spearheads his economic development efforts, to monitor Daewoosa and make sure they follow all the rules. "I would prefer not to have the federal government be in charge of monitoring local places of employment," Tauese said. "They have their own way of doing things and our interests and theirs are not always the same."

—*Samoa News,* March 15, 2000

I was just beginning to understand that cultural differences ran deeper than I had ever imagined, and my logic, however well-founded, held little sway over time-honored ritual. I was a mostly white woman representing a disenfranchised group of Asians on an island populated by Polynesians.

One afternoon in mid-March of 2000, Christa, Rob, and I were at Dale and Adeline's house meeting with some of our clients. Hoa was in the kitchen, singing with a radio and cooking tiny egg rolls. Several of the workers cooked, but Hoa was the paramount chef. She could organize teams of chopping sous chefs and whip out a fantastic, multicourse Vietnamese meal in a few hours. Hoa dressed in short skirts and tight shirts and looked you in the face when she spoke to you. Since she was taller, larger, and louder than most of the women, this caught your attention. She was one of the first workers to put light-brown streaks in her jet-black hair, and I used to see sparkles on her skin.

Quyen was helping her in the kitchen. Quyen, like most of the workers, was in her early twenties. She had straight black chin-length hair that she wore parted in the middle, and she crossed her hands in front of her in a way that divided her, like the part in her hair. I found her shy and deferential, like many of the others; but I later discovered that it was just the language barrier than made her appear so. Like her coworkers, she was in fact one of the most intrepid clients with whom I've worked, even though she spoke softly.

Tam and Gam and Taller Thuy were on the lanai, playing with the kittens that had been born the past fall. Gam was around one hundred pounds when she arrived in American Samoa, and it appeared that she was even tinier lately. Even so, she was a striking woman and seemed to be all huge dark eyes. She was more guarded and considered in her responses, and when she spoke it was deliberate.

Tam was holding two kittens and laughing, her eyes sparkling. She was a regular at our meetings and was a solid part of the "core" group of plaintiffs. Tam conveyed balance and when I was with her, I could better feel the floor. She learned to understand English long before she let on, and was adept at appreciating nuance. She also was a keen observer and would enable us to better understand the events that took place within the Daewoosa compound.

Hung, one of our few male worker clients, was on the porch, smoking. He had a great deal of gumption and was not as measured in his speech as the majority of the women. He was far more outspoken, and less afraid to speak directly to Lee. Rumor had it that his family was well-off, financially and politically, in Vietnam. Hung incessantly smoked Benson & Hedges menthols and talked and gestured constantly with his hands about the injustices at the factory. He was also taking English lessons from Bill Hyman, one of the kindest and most interested members of the Concerned Citizen's Coalition.

Nga was telling us the story of the twenty-two hundred seventy-four dollar Department of Labor-ordered settlement money. Dung was translating. Christa and I were taking notes.

It appeared that in September 1999 the Department of Labor settlement checks were distributed one afternoon to twenty workers. Robert Atimalala, one of the Samoan managers at the factory, offered to drive the workers to the local bank so they could cash them. The women piled into the Daewoosa van and headed off to the Amerika Samoa Bank. Spirits were high; these workers had not been paid regular wages for months. They were discussing how to spend the money, and most planned to send the bulk of it back to their families in Vietnam. Nga, in particular, was excited to send money to her family—they badly needed it.

The workers arrived at the bank, went inside, and lined up at the teller window. Robert Atimalala accompanied the first woman up to the teller window, to ease the language difference, Nga thought. The woman handed the teller the check and received her $2,274. Just like that, Robert Atimalala reached over and snatched that wad of money away from her! He put the cash in his pocket and motioned for the next worker to come to the teller window.

The remaining women turned and fled. No fools, they. Apparently, Lee had forbidden the women to return to work unless they coughed up the twenty-two hundred seventy-four dollar settlement money over to him. Four of the workers gave their settlement money to Lee, and those four kept working. The remaining sixteen workers were not allowed to work in the factory. Appallingly, the $2,274 received in September 1999 was the only wage received by those workers for many months. These funds had seriously dwindled by March 2000, and the workers were very concerned.

Dale, Robert, and I went out on the porch, underneath Mount Alava. It is better for one to look up when in Pago Pago. It has the most well-protected harbor in the South Pacific and was home to two large commercial tuna canneries. The green jungle that covered the towering mountains is a much more beautiful sight than the mundane streets below. Rob and I had Vailima beers and Dale had a glass of water. Dale was a tall, attractive palagi with receding gray hair. He had a sharp, incisive wit and a room became more charged when he entered. He and Adeline were trying desperately to get Dung into the United States, but since she was a Vietnamese citizen this was somewhat daunting. They had communicated extensively with people that Dale knew in Washington, DC, from his Department of Interior days. Dung was no longer working at Daewoosa and also wanted to go to the United States so she could attend school, but she was receiving pressure from her family in Vietnam. Dung's mother had apparently already spent two years in prison—two years!—for not paying back a loan. Dung's sister worked at Tour Company 12, one of the "management" companies that brought the workers to the territory to labor at Daewoosa. I put quotation marks around "management"—these companies answered to the Vietnam National Administration of Tourism and the Vietnam Ministry of Labour, War Invalid, and Social Affairs. They were part of the Vietnamese government, as near as we could tell.

The pressure put on the workers' families in Vietnam was incredible. Earlier that afternoon, one of the workers showed us a letter received recently from a cousin in Vietnam. It said, in part:

I am in utter confusion with news from all sources coming from Samoa, and some sounded serious, grim, and troubling. When I got a call from your father today, I was like a drowning person who just got a buoy. He said you told him everything is all right.

No matter what happens at the workplace, try to believe that you'll survive as you promised me and your father on the second floor of my house, the night before you left. I am thirty-six years old now, and in living in thirty-six years, life has taught me this: be enduring, calm, and alert, and you will be successful.

It is been more than a year since Vietnam signed any contract with foreign countries to export labor, even though the unemployed are so many, which causes social illness. In the midst of all this a contract for exporting labor to Samoa is the best relief available and has been evaluated by the Ministry of Labor along with IMS. Tour Company 12, where I work, and a number of others who have the ability to export labor are involved. If there is no change, they will get permission to send people to American Samoa; thus soon, there will not be just a few dozen people like your group but there will be hundreds of professional sewing workers or at least those who are properly trained being sent over, recruited by the real Koreans—not mixed-matched like your group.

If you were mistakenly participating in or organizing a demonstration, strike, or thinking of escaping, please think again. Don't make IMS think poorly of me and my company. I may have to sell my house to pay for your debt; however, that pain is not anywhere to be compared with the loss of my job if IMS takes action against me because of you—a cousin of mine—and talks to the leader of my company. In that case, I will be in big trouble. Moreover, think about the nation's reputation. Do not make this incident scare people away, so nobody wants to cooperate with Vietnamese anymore. If the employer annuls the contract, hundreds, thousands, even a million workers may lose their opportunity to have a job. In fact, workers have long complained about the Korean contacts, which treated workers harshly; yet millions of workers in Asia—not only Vietnamese but also the Filipinos and Chinese—are competing for their jobs. At the same time, there is evidence that the export labor contracts signed with Korean employers have been proven economically satisfactory to the Vietnamese workers. Where is the conflict?

Please do not forget under any circumstances: let

me and your family hear from you. I have not broken this news to your parents for I am not sure it is true or not and I do not want to see my relative suffering and bending their heads down because of shame.

This letter had been passed among the workers and caused no small amount of alarm. I had no idea of the scale of shaming one's family in Vietnam—it was a most grievous harm. Now here was something I could not imagine. I had been encouraged by my parents to speak out, to seek justice, to stand up for those who had no voice. Here, instead, the workers' families threatened to "disown" them, to excise them from reputable familial status. This was incredibly hard for me to grasp. I thus began to get a glimmering of the vast differences in United States' and Vietnamese cultures. I had thought I understood diversity; I assumed I had enough in common with others to appreciate different beliefs and attitudes. Once again, I didn't know the magnitude of what I didn't know. (This theme continues to follow me, for all its good and ill.) I couldn't identify in the least with a family who might be shamed by actions their child considered right and true—especially seeking payment for work done as promised. I had expected every single worker to join the suit in droves and was surprised to see that, initially, there was much trepidation about how such a legal confrontation would play in Vietnam.

Dale and I were talking about the future of the case. It was slowly becoming apparent to me that this was one great big can of worms. We were still handling the case pro bono at that time, and the time and logistic requirements were getting difficult for me. U'una'i offered free legal services for victims of domestic violence, and we were swamped on a calm day. I was working long days and into the nights for the U'una'i clients and trying to handle 250-plus Daewoosa workers at other times. I whined a bit to Dale about the situation and the language problem on top of all else. He listened patiently and occasionally winked at Rob and offered him another beer. Since he and Adeline were also teaching Dung English, we had talked with her about acting as a translator in court, but thus far she was unsure of her interpretation abilities and hesitant to do so. The translation problem in court was off-putting: Lee was no fool when he chose Vietnamese workers to come to the Territory of American Samoa. The territory's Asian communities include Chinese, Korean, Filipino, Japanese—but no Vietnamese. We were unable to find one Vietnamese-speaking person on our seventeen-mile-long island. Not one!

"It's daunting, is all," I said.

Dale chuckled. "Like life."

"Mm. But where's it going? I feel like we're hitting wall after wall, and Lee is just ignoring what the court has ordered! And what's right."

"So what do you want to do, quit?" Dale took a sip of his water and gazed out over Pago Pago Harbor.

"Well no, no, not quit, but ..."

"Then there is only one thing to do." He looked kindly at me, and I was aware of how much he had seen and learned in his life, and it sparked out like a calming light. Everyone on the island seemed to heartily like and respect Dale; he got along without making enemies. He endured the frustrating and idiosyncratic local customs with humor, somehow, and without compromising his own notions.

"You keep on trying, and keep on the next day and the next." He held up his water glass, and we clinked it with our beer bottles. "Besides," he said, winking, "we never know what the future will bring."

Now that word of the lawsuit had gotten back to Vietnam, some of the other workers were receiving criticism from their families back in Vietnam, and pressure to stop all the heretical fuss. They were doubly motivated, to be sure: they were the very families who had paid Tour Company 12 or IMS those hefty recruiting fees.

At first we thought that many of the workers brought to the territory were from families who were relatively well-off financially. This turned out not to be so, although they did possess the savvy to know where to find the money. However, this led to a number of workers coming to the territory who were less than expert seamstresses. The workers were required to take some sort of a sewing test before they were accepted to come to Daewoosa. They told us that the test was simple; the real test was ponying up thousands of dollars.

Many of the workers' families mortgaged their homes and sold their possessions to get the money for Tour Company 12 and IMS. The chance that one of their family members would get the opportunity to go to the United States and earn money and all that implied was irresistible, and it held the glittery promise of all such dreams.

Christa and I met on a sunny Saturday morning in late-March of 2000 on the porch of the little yellow house. She had no car then and took the bus to the bottom of our mountain but had to walk up the long and winding perforated paved driveway up to the house. It was a beautiful but very steep walk through jungle, and occasionally you could see through the trees to

Faga'alu Bay below. If the tide was low the water was turquoise and the shallow coral reef dotted the bay. Tropic birds swooped and danced in the air high above the water, and showed up bright white against the green of the jutting mountains. I always watched them closely, mindful that someone had once told me that they could fly backward. I never did see that, but I still think it could happen.

"Water," Christa whispered when she approached the house. "Give me water." She was walking hard and fanning herself with her ubiquitous hat.

"Here! Buck up!" I ran and got her a tall glass of water. It was exceptionally hot and sunny that day; it hadn't rained yet. I came back out on the porch as Christa collapsed onto a chair. "Our water is out again," I noted.

"Where did you get this?" She held up the glass in her hand.

"Bottled. And getting pricier, because we don't have water for *anything*, like the bathroom or showers or dishes."

"So what's the prob?" She was already looking perkier.

"Something up at Rose's pump or tank." Rose, our landlady, was an ancient and respected matriarch on the island and she lived about a quarter mile above us on the mountain. She came from an old and powerful family and was the eldest of many sisters. She owned the mountain. The Faga'alu village chiefs might object, but she paid them no mind and continued owning the mountain. She was not known to be free with her money and would often refuse to spend the teeniest bit on structural repairs or maintenance. This tended to infuriate her tenants. She built the little yellow house, for example, with untreated wood, no foundation, and cheap workers, and now the walls were being eaten away by rot and termites. The water issue, although vexing, was not uncommon.

"Did you bring the contract?" I asked Christa.

"Yep." She pulled it out of her book bag. "The contracts are all between 'USA Daewoosa Co., Ltd.,' the employer, and

'Tour Company 12,' the labor supply company. Daewoosa's local PO box and phone number are listed, as is Tour Company 12's in Vietnam. It also provides that the workers will be paid at the basic salary of $408 per month. I think that's because they figured minimum wage for seamstresses in the territory is $2.60 per hour. However, they based that $408 on a four-week month, so they're already in violation of local minimum wages laws."

"Does it provide for periods when there is no work available to the workers?" I wondered about this.

"It does. I'll read it: 'Said wages shall be paid ... in the case that the worker does not work by reason not caused by them. [For example, short of electricity, material, etc.] The basic wages would be paid to the workers by Daewoosa.'"

"So the workers should have been paid consistently, even if the factory had no material or no outstanding orders." I thought that made sense.

"Right. There is just nothing good about Lee or Daewoosa."

"Does the contract provide for payment of FICA and ASG withholding tax?"

"Sure does. It mandates a 2 percent withholding for the tax, and 7.65 percent for FICA. Both to be taken out and paid by the employer, Daewoosa."

"And we don't know if they've even made those payments?" I made a note to look into whether those payments were current.

"Nope."

"What do you reckon?" I answered sarcastically. "The American Samoa government sure doesn't seem to care about what they do at the factory."

Christa shrugged. She had a fabulous way of shrugging and dismissing at the same time; she still does. "The contract also sets out the responsibilities of both parties. Weirdly, it also dictates that the workers' wages are to be paid to Tour Company 12's bank account, in Vietnam!"

"What? That's too bizarre for words."

"It also provides for arbitration in the event of any dispute arising during the execution of the contract. But I like this provision: 'In case the workers work "uncontentedly," as they had higher expectation due to the party B's misguidance made before they leave Vietnam, they will be dismissed.'"

"Nice syntax. 'Work uncontentedly'? Like they whine?" I was all over that.

Christa shot me a look. "I guess. Or maybe when they refuse to work?"

"Still seems a tad vague to me, legally."

We continued picking through the contract. It reflected only the relationship between Daewoosa and the management companies. Thus far, we hadn't seen any contracts between the workers and the defendants. Nga and Dung had told us that they each had theirs and would bring them to us soon. Christa and I were interested in discovering what parallels existed between the two—or more—sets of contracts.

"By the way, congratulations on your election, Virginia!" Christa raised her water glass.

"Thanks." The past week I had been elected president of the American Samoa Bar Association. "It lends a bit of credibility when I'm asked to speak." Also counteracts the likelihood that I had been asked to speak for comic relief, I didn't add.

As project director for U'una'i, I had been asked to speak at most of the domestic violence workshops or seminars in the territory. Domestic violence was just now emerging as a potentially bad thing in American Samoa. For example, one morning I was out for an early morning walk. While on a public sidewalk walking through the village of Fagatogo, I had come upon a man repeatedly smacking a woman on the shoulders and head. I went over to them and told him to stop, right now. He looked at me, shook his head, and attempted to reassure me. "It's *okay*," he explained patiently, softly, like to a child. "She's my *wife*." To his credit, he did stop short of patting me on the head.

Although people educated off-island tended to think in broader and more enlightened terms, hitting seemed as good a response as any to many of the residents of Tutuila. Withholding one's salary was another, and adultery was not uncommon (although probably not more so than anywhere else: we just lived on a tiny island and knew everybody's business). This would become an issue later in the case when the Daewoosa ladies would be portrayed as less than respectable.

Adultery was considered a problem by some of the local politicians. At a recent session of the Fono, a representative submitted a bill that would make adultery carry a civil penalty. As part of the bill, all tinted windows on vehicles on the island would be outlawed, since inside them was where most of the adultery went on. He referred to the tinted glass as "adultery windows."

Mostly, though, spouses got hit, and more often than not it was the women. Many of the notions about abuse—and divorce—were new to the territory. Most of my clients were convinced that they could not obtain a divorce unless their spouses consented. Most thought their husbands would get custody of the children because he was the one working outside the home and had the money. They were astounded when they found out they could receive spousal and child support. It was such a delicious trip to present *options* to people who had thought they had none, who had never considered even the notion that they had a choice. The federal government paid me in money for my job, and my clients paid me in hugs, Samoan food, art, and babies named Virginia and Robert.

Even though the government wouldn't grant me money to represent the Vietnamese women as sufferers of domestic violence, I still thought of the case in those terms. There was a pattern here. The more we learned about the predicament of our clients, from the condition of the factory, to the heartbreaking pressure from their families at home in Vietnam, the more our resolve hardened to prevent any further harm to them, to teach them about their options, and to help reclaim what they'd earned. The resolve would be tested many times.

CHAPTER FIVE—SPEAK TRUTH TO POWER

We suffered a major emotional and unexpected setback when, the following month, Dale Jones died in his sleep. We attended the funeral service, along with most of the island population; Dale was extremely well-liked and respected. He was a calm and calming man. He and Adeline had welcomed the workers into their home and their hearts. The workers understood the allies they had in Dale and Adeline.

The workers were distraught at Dale's unexpected death. Adeline was as steadfast and regal a friend they could find and continued to offer her house as a place of refuge for all the Daewoosa workers.

The workers were becoming engaged and invested in the lawsuit. Over the months, we had become more and more concerned about the workers' lack of nutritious food as provided by the factory. It was apparent that food was not high on Kil-Soo Lee's priority list. In fact, it may not have even been on the list.

Christa and I found Dr. Heather Margaret at the LBJ Medical Center. She and her husband, Mike, were godsends to the island, and to our case. Dr. Heather was an extraordinarily bright, cheerful, dogged woman who had practiced medicine in primarily low-income places in the United States. She was keenly tuned in to nutrition issues and was the first to raise questions about the workers' weight loss. The women were small to begin with, but she pointed out they were getting smaller. They needed a proper diet.

The workers responded to this need as best they could. Most had made friends with local families (mostly Samoan but also palagi). Here is how some of these liaisons began.

The workers would group outside stores and markets. They would come up to shoppers and press a piece of paper into their hands. The paper was soft from being folded many times and held in countless sweaty little palms. The paper had words on it, in English; "magic words." The paper did not ask for money, even though the women had not received a paycheck in months. The paper asked if the worker could clean your house, or sweep your yard, or cook a meal for your family. For a few dollars, please.

They congregated outside many of the local stores, including the newly opened Cost-U-Less (locally known as the Cost-U-More). I heard that one day Justice Richmond and his wife came to the store to shop. And the workers handed *him* their little sweaty paper.

The most beneficial effect to come out of those inquiries was that many of the workers—maybe as many as two-thirds—were embraced and "adopted" by a local Samoan or palagi family. Many, many of them were brought to the island homes and given food, emotional support, and chores for a bit of money. Christa called them our clients' safe homes, and they were. For all the world, it seemed like the islanders were sympathetic with the workers' predicament.

But the Daewoosa workers were still going to bed hungry. They simply were not provided sufficient food at the compound. We filed another order to show cause motion against Kil-Soo Lee to force him to feed the workers decent meals that were up to nutritional standards. After all, the contracts they signed had stated they would be provided three meals a day. However, Lee refused to follow the contract and feed them adequately, so we were forced to take him to court to enforce that.

This is the vexing thing about the justice system: it is slow. I chose to believe that its slowness is a result of its focus on preserving due process and the rights of all litigants. I know it is slow—but better slow than wrong, in my opinion. We had taken Lee to court regularly but had yet to see actual dollars in our clients' pockets or food on their tables. We were months away from taking this to trial (we were still gathering information), but the workers needed food *now*.

The workers protested in their quiet ways. They met on the garment factory grounds and discussed the case. They did not hide their dismayed attitudes toward Daewoosa management. One day, police came to the factory compound and took Nga and Hung to the Tafuna police substation. The complaint, filed by Daewoosa management, alleged they were "making trouble."

DAEWOOSA SAMOA WORKERS TAKE BOSSES TO COURT AGAIN

"If [Daewoosa Samoa] expects to do business on American soil, they'd better expect to live by our laws rather than foreign laws," declared Associate Justice Lyle Richmond last Friday afternoon after an expedited hearing in the High Court.

This time, workers' attorneys Virginia Lynn Sudbury and Christa Lin asked the High Court for an injunction to prevent Daewoosa managers from interfering with the workers' first amendment rights of free speech and peaceable assembly.

Other Daewoosa tidbits gleaned at the hearing:

Daewoosa president/owner Mr. Kil-Soo Lee does

not speak English and required an English-to-Korean translator during the hearing, although he never did seem to require one during previous court hearings.

Ms. Nga told of being threatened with being summarily returned to Vietnam if her name is not removed from the class-action suit.

"Yes, I am afraid to be here today," in this courtroom, she told the court. "We believe that maybe something bad will happen to us" because of the lawsuit.

"But I believe that when we did the lawsuit, we do the right thing, and I keep my name on the lawsuit," she added.

—Samoa News, July 10, 2000

The lawsuit received a growing amount of international publicity, primarily from other islands in the South Pacific. Most of it was unfavorable toward the American Samoa government. The governor made outraged speeches and eschewed responsibility; Christa and I were not complimented; in fact, we were blamed. Members of the public accused the American Samoa government of complacency toward the workers' plight, at best. Things were getting ugly.

Lee's anger toward the lawsuit and everyone related to it was increasing. One evening we received an urgent telephone call from Adeline Jones, who related that Lee had just purchased airline tickets for two of the workers—Mr. Hung and Ms. Hang—and was attempting to send them back to Vietnam against their will (and against the court's orders). Lee was punishing Hung for his visible and vocal involvement in the lawsuit and was punishing Hang because she was pregnant. We filed for an emergency show cause hearing and alleged that Lee again violated the court's earlier injunction against interfering with the plaintiffs.

HOUSE COMMITTEE HEARS ABOUT DAEWOOSA'S PREGNANT WORKERS

A court injunction earlier this year prevented Daewoosa Samoa from sending one of two pregnant Vietnamese workers back to her homeland, according to testimony before the House Rules Committee two days ago.

The woman has since given birth to twins who are now being cared for by the Nazareth House staff at Fatu-O-Aiga. Whether she is still working at Daewoosa was not disclosed during the hearing.

The birth of the twins has raised a serious concern among lawmakers and the public over the issue that these two children are now US nationals, having been born on American soil.

OTHER PUBLIC COMPLAINTS

Rep. Muavaefa'atasi Ae Ae Jr. revealed during the hearing that some of the Vietnamese women are going to nightclubs and other places considered unsafe for them.

He noted that possible pregnancies from these social activities will cause problems for American Samoa in the future.

Muavaefa'atasi believes that maybe it's time to amend local laws to prevent foreign workers, such as

Daewoosa's case from coming here and giving birth and having their children become US nationals.

—*Samoa News*, July 21, 2000

In the course of investigating this, we discovered that Lee had also banned Nga and several *other* workers from the factory and was attempting to force them out of the territory through intimidation tactics. The workers tended more toward leaving the compound and staying with their "safe" families. They returned to sew and sleep.

It seemed like any Daewoosa surface we scratched revealed more bad behavior on Lee's part. The workers, Christa, and I trooped back to court and presented yet more evidence of Lee's intrusions, including copies of the flight manifest procured from the local airline showing he had willfully violated the court's last order and intended to deport Hung and Hang. The court agreed and Lee was admonished.

Each of these hearings produced more courageous testimony from our Vietnamese workers. The court agreed with us, and Hung and Hang did not have to go back to Vietnam. This was fortunate, as Hang was eight months' pregnant. The court also stated that Lee and Daewoosa had violated the terms of the earlier injunction, held them in contempt, and issued a supplementary injunction. Lee was fined, but as he left the courtroom, he flashed his trademark smirk and his expensive silk suit and matching two-toned shoes, and we knew that our struggle was far from over.

Whenever I heard of Lee's latest transgressions, my professional modus operandi was to shoo everyone out of my office, close my door, and vent loudly. Since the walls are not very thick, this venting was heard by all and sundry in the outer offices. This behavior alarmed no one, although Mark Ude, one of our lawyers, suggested I get a "Virginia doll." It would be just like the Chatty Cathy doll of the sixties, only when the Virginia doll's string was pulled, she would shout, "But he can't *do* that!"

I was clearly beginning to have a hard time in paradise. I had honestly thought I tolerated and understood cultural differences on a core level. I was after all from the east coast. Now I wasn't so sure about my broadmindedness. I figured there were some commonalities with life on the US mainland, such as, for instance, in the area of medical care.

"Patients have already died unnecessarily in the recent past," said the chief executive officer of the LBJ Tropical Medical Center. The lack of timely payment by LBJ to off-island vendors has caused vendors to suspend shipments to LBJ, and as a result LBJ is now entering a critical period as regards the hospital's ability to treat its patients.

—*Samoa News,* November 27, 1996

The LBJ Tropical Medical Center was the American Samoan version of a hospital. Unfortunately, LBJ was run by the American Samoa government and as such, was subject to extreme misappropriation of monies, serious financial woes, and all manner of medical tomfoolery. The tropics also wreaked havoc on equipment. It's not that the ASG didn't get plenty of money from the US government—they received millions of dollars per year from the feds. The problem was that the money somehow didn't get to all the places it was supposed to, including LBJ. This led to the obvious loosening of standards. I am sure this happens all over the world, but all over the world didn't affect me directly.

I went to LBJ for my annual pap smear, something I consider a less-than-festive occasion under the best of circumstances, and LBJ was certainly not the best. After the exam, the Samoan nurse practitioner took out her questionnaire and asked me if I had any history of cancer in my family.

"I don't know—I'm adopted," I replied.

"But what about the mother?"

"I don't know—I haven't talked with my *birth* mother."

"But what about the sisters and the brothers?" She tapped the clipboard with her pen impatiently. "I need to fill up the space."

"I don't know them. I don't know anyone I'm blood related to."

"But the babies?"

"I don't have any babies." She looked at me like I was a piece of bad cheese. I pressed on through the judgmental silence.

"So when do I get the results of my test?" I asked her. "Do you analyze the test on-island?"

"No, no, it goes to the lab in Hawaii."

"How long does it take?" I needed to structure my worrying.

The nurse practitioner hemmed and hawed for what seemed to be a great long time. Now I was thinking that something was wrong with the test. "How long does it take to get the results?" I pressed.

"Because ASG pays the Hawaii lab to do the test, and the ASG has not paid yet."

"Ah." I was getting it now. "How far behind is the ASG in payments?"

She shrugged. "Eight, maybe nine months."

"You mean there are nine months' of pap smears stacking up in some lab in Hawaii? And all these women here on-island are waiting for results?"

She nodded sadly at the floor. "Yes." Then she looked up, brightly. "Do you mind the wait?"

I did indeed. I snatched the pap smear slide out of her hand, stuck it in my purse, and stormed out. It remained in my purse for the better part of a week while I tracked down a laboratory in Hawaii that would read the results and let me pay directly. It gave me a strangely empowered feeling, arguing in front of the High Court and knowing I had a pap smear in my handbag.

I can also personally attest that the hospital substituted medications without notifying patients. Not that a good portion of the blame wasn't user error. Several years prior I visited the LBJ pharmacy to pick up an anti-inflammatory medication. They were out of that particular medication and gave me a substitution. I took it for a week before I found out it was prostate cancer medicine. (Now *that's* an affliction I can cross off my worry list.) I went back to LBJ and loudly demanded to see the pharmacist. I was hurriedly shunted into the backroom to wait (and to stop alarming the other patients, no doubt). While I cooled my heels, I noticed a 1982 copy of the *Physician's Desk Reference* lying open on the desk. (This was in 1997.) The glossy and colorful page on anti-inflammatory medications had been ripped out of the book and was folded into a paper airplane, just sitting there waiting to fly.

Kathleen Kolhoff was our intrepid grant writer, wise counselor, and dear friend. It was she who wrote the original grants to establish U'una'i, and it was her encouraging words that kept us convinced it was a worthy endeavor. She was a tenured professor at American Samoa Community College (ASCC), taught English, and headed the drama department. Her students, under her keen and creative direction, produced several eagerly anticipated plays every year. Kathleen is an extraordinarily lively and striking woman, with red hair that hangs to her waist and an attitude that matches her hair color. She has played the role of Sadie in Somerset Maugham's *Rain* on the island several times: there is no one better than Kathleen to bring Sadie to life (not even Joan Crawford).

She is also a mom. Kathleen adopted Fisaga at birth, and they are a close and companionable team. Fisaga is a curious and tenacious girl with her mother's sense of self-confidence. At this time, they lived in a little pink house in one of the small villages on the island, and everyone who knew Kathleen and Fisaga liked them.

But March 1, 2000, was a bad day. Around four o'clock that morning Kathleen woke up in the bed she shared with four-year-old Fisaga to find a man holding a knife to her throat. He raped her while Fisaga watched. He told Kathleen that she was his girlfriend. She picked up on that theme and convinced him she would meet him later that day, when they had more time. This took some convincing dialogue but Kathleen could persuade the devil himself (as she did in this case). The bad man believed her and took her jewelry and left. Kathleen scooped up Fisaga in her arms and sprinted just as fast as she could to her neighbor's house, forgetting they had just laid a new cement front porch. She hit that new sharp cement edge running and flew into the front door, breaking both her feet. She also broke Fisaga's fall. The neighbors sprang into action and wove an emotionally supportive net around Kathleen and Fisaga; one with hugs and protection and justified outrage and comforting food and telephone calls to the police.

I was in High Court later that morning for a trial. I had begun my opening statement when Rob came before the bar and whispered what had happened with Kathleen and that she was asking for me from the hospital. I approached the chief justice

Virginia Lynn Sudbury

62

and he let us continue the trial until another day; he was very generous in that.

I arrived at the hospital (and to the same department where I had enjoyed the pap smear antics several weeks prior). I told them I needed to see Kathleen and they asked if I were her mother and I said no, her sister, and they let me back. She looked freaked out but her grit was doing the talking. She wanted to go immediately home and write up the report for the police so they could catch the bad man. Ten minutes later, she was in her home on her computer detailing the ghastly events of the morning and her incredibly detailed description of the bad man, a cigarette dangling from her lips and a resolute look in her eye. Thoughtfully, she included a detailed description of his "teeny, weenie dick."

Later that morning the police caught the bad man. They caught him at the place Kathleen had earlier and shrewdly arranged to meet him. He had her jewelry with him. The police arrested the bad man and took him to the territorial prison. The public defender was appointed to represent him. Tafi and Tua, the three-hundred-pound investigators with the public defender's office picked up the bad man at the prison in their vehicle to transport him to the court the morning of his hearing.

Somehow, though, the bad man arrived at his arraignment bleeding and covered with fresh-looking bruises. We asked what happened, and Tua shook his head sorrowfully and said, "Oh, Virginia. Because we turned the corners. Tafi must have fallen against him in the car. Too bad, huh?"

No one messes with Kathleen.

High Court of American Samoa

Nguyen Thi Nga

Virginia meeting with workers

In loving memory of our beautiful, wonderful, and courageous daughters and sisters,

Nguyen Thi Nga & Dung Kim Thi Vu

who were swept out to sea on August 27, 2000. May they rest in peace, wherever they may be.

A memorial gathering will be held at Ma & Pa Jones' house in Malaloa on September 2, 2000 at 10:00 a.m. to commemorate the exceptional lives of these two young women.

Dung Vu and Nguyen Thi Nga are survived by many who loved and cared for them.

For more information, please call Ms. Virginia Lynn Sudbury at 699-2892 or Ms. Christa Lin at 258-1137.

SAMOA NEWS   25 August 2000

Memorial Nga and Dung

Sliding Rock

Incarcerated injured workers

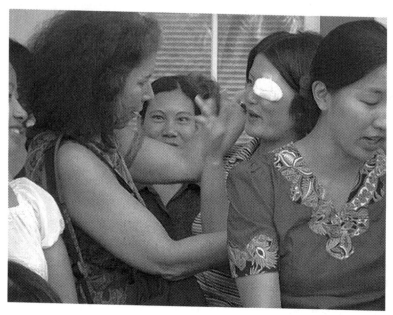

Virginia, Hoa, Quyen and Christa on High Court Porch

**Clockwise from right: Tam, Quyen,
Virginia, Hoa, Christa**

Chapter Six—Walking Spanish

One morning a few weeks later, Hung arrived at our office breathless and excited. After dark the night before, a few workers had covertly pawed through the factory dumpster and discovered a "direct order" issued by the Vietnam National Administration of Tourism. It was dated April 25, 2000, and was addressed to Comrade Minh, Lee's Vietnamese crony in "charge" and all of the Vietnamese workers. The direct order commanded the workers to drop the lawsuit and stated, "We know there will be another court hearing on 5/5/2000 over the same old subject as before. We order you to stop everything. You must not appear in court on this date. If you do not obey this order you are breaking the law. Anyone who disobeys this order must pay the consequences to Daewoosa Company and Tourism Company 12."

We finally had something in writing from Vietnam! This document would be invaluable to establishing the relationship between Daewoosa and Vietnam. While this helped our case, it also terrified the workers. Their families were still back in Vietnam and were ultimately liable for their behavior—and for the "breach" of contracts that would ensue. The negative impact on their lives and on those of their families could not be overestimated.

In the summer of 2000, six months into the case, Lee's lawyer, Malaetasi Togafau, quit and was replaced by Aitofele Sunia, the brother of Governor Tauese Sunia. The procedural aspects of the case became more twisted as the days went by. We suspected unsavory government involvement and filed requests for discovery and production of documents and set a date for deposing Lee. Lee responded by filing a motion for protective order to enjoin the discovery and succeeded in delaying matters several weeks; but the court ultimately upheld our discovery requests. We asked for everything that had to do with the Daewoosa factory: operation, ownership, investors, insurers, bank accounts. We requested the tests and applications that Lee used in Vietnam that initially facilitated the workers to enter the sewing employment contracts. We requested the contracts that Lee had made them sign in Vietnam—and the subsequent contracts that Malaetasi made them sign on the plane as it flew east over the Pacific to Tutuila. We argued that these were in fact adhesion contracts and added them to our litany of bad acts committed by Kil-Soo Lee. Those contracts lowered their wages and imposed greater restrictions. The workers were uneasy about signing the new contracts on the airplane but their choices were somewhat limited. They had no legal counsel and no representatives. They could sign the new contract or be deported back to Vietnam as soon as the plane landed in Pago Pago. It raised nibbles of concern, but surely they were being overcautious. They had been promised; America had the "chances." They signed.

"You owe allegiance to this administration. You are an extension of us. You have no private right to criticize

the policy of this administration publicly." Governor
Tauese Sunia.

—*Samoa News,* September 27, 1997

Meanwhile, tropical life in Pago Pago in the year 2000 went on.
We worked a lot. I enjoyed our little yellow house and sitting
and working on the porch overlooking the harbor. Truly, that
was one beautiful view. Our landlady Rose's banana plantation
surrounded our property, running right below the porch and
around the edge of the yard and extending several hundred feet
down to the road, next to the sea. We had a small yard around
the yellow house that was maintained by Fitu and Kisa, two
young women who did yard work and housework for Ms. Rose.
They moved in slow motion and oftentimes wore elaborate
cover (shirts tied over their faces, and lampshades) when they
worked in the garden. They wore boxes on their legs when they
weed-whacked to protect their legs from flying rocks. They
weed-whacked everything, including our series of inflatable
wading pools. I once noticed them sitting, motionless, in the
banana plantation, so still as to become part of the foliage.

They were from western Samoa and were thin and strong.
They were remotely related to Ms. Rose but apparently weren't
all that enthusiastic about leaving their home and families in
order to move to Pago Pago to wait on Ms. Rose, who could be
snappish. Once, Kisa hopped the thirty-minute flight to Apia
and ran back to her family, but Ms. Rose went right over to Apia
herself and gave money to the family and brought Kisa back.
This time she kept her passport.

I still went on my walks, even though people still looked at
me askance. One day in early summer I was walking through
Fagatogo. I heard someone yelling. I recognized the voice as
belonging to Hertrudes. She was sitting cross-legged on the

ground and engaged in an animated discussion with a local dog. I didn't want to make her uncomfortable and walked on by. It seemed as if the sun was only visiting in the trees. I looked back and could've sworn that dog turned and grinned at me.

I started taking an aerobics class. It was held at Herb and Sia's Hotel in the village of Faga'alu. The class took place in a big room with mirrors on the main floor of the hotel. Sadly for us exercisers, though, that big room also housed the hotel bar; so we jumped up and down in a smoky haze amid an ongoing commentary from the bar patrons. I really didn't understand much about aerobics; I was a swimmer, but I gamely tried to follow along. Our instructor, Roberta, had lots of energy and a wonderful New Zealand accent. I missed a lot of what she said, but I understood enough to know that when she said "leeeg," I was to fling my leg in a certain direction, and so forth.

Robbie took up golf.

WHAT WERE THE POLICE DOING AT THE ILI'ILI GOLF COURSE ON SATURDAY?

Dear Just Asking,

According to informed sources, newly confirmed director of parks and recreation has joined forces with our local department of public safety to ensure that golfers pay the greens fees before they are allowed to play. Police officers were stationed at the golf course from six a.m. until two p.m. to assist golf course employees and make certain the fees were paid.

—*Samoa News,* November 15, 1997

We got cable television on the island. Before that we just had the two channels, both of which were owned and operated by the ASG. One of the channels came on at noon and one at six in the evening and neither operated past midnight. We got cable but soon found out the shows were taped on the mainland, physically sent to the island in the form of videos, and replayed. Because of the transportation delay, they were generally replayed two weeks late. This made for oddly timed postholiday television. The mainland seemed farther and farther away.

Cocounsel Christa Lin and I were called to testify before the Fono on the status of the Daewoosa case. We were ushered into the hushed, stately chamber of the legislature, Daewoosa files and notes in hand, and were instructed to sit at the end of the long circular table. We had chosen our local hand-sewn outfits carefully and with an eye not to offend, but it was difficult for me not to visibly scowl back at what I perceived as a paternalistic, misogynistic, culturally elitist gathering. The session was called to order and we faced a semicircle of stern and unsmiling Samoan lawmakers. All were male. They did not look happy to see us.

The congressmen commenced with openly hostile questioning about our Vietnamese clients. They asked nothing about Lee or the factory or the merits of the case itself. The congressmen accused our clients of stealing fruit from trees, of looking for other employment, of freely walking about the island, and of "inviting" incidents of sexual assault. The lawmakers angrily pointed out that if our clients were allowed to walk around the island at night, they might be raped! Why didn't we keep our clients locked in the compound at night? the congressmen wanted to know. Oh, and by the way, this fuss was making American Samoa look bad in the eyes of the world; and that was our fault.

Christa and I swallowed our pride and gave our oft-repeated spiel about the conditions in which the workers lived, the lack of food and privacy, and most about Lee's failure to pay the workers. The lawmakers did not address those issues; the after-dark excursions by our clients were their sole concerns. Christa boldly pointed out that *she* walked around after dark, and were the congressmen equally concerned about her being raped? They appeared confused by the question. Several frowned at us, as if we had behaved inappropriately. Christa pointed out further that our clients possessed every right that the congressmen themselves had. "Oh, no," several shouted, "oh, no, they certainly do not, and you can't tell us that because we know it isn't true." They were mad at us after that, madder than before, and disgusted.

One bright afternoon that summer, long tables were set up in front of the main factory building on the Daewoosa compound. Chairs were set up on one side of the tables, and several factory managers filed in with stacks of papers and sat down. They announced that the workers would be paid immediately. The managers ceremoniously called out names and handed paychecks out to the workers. Everyone was happy at first, until the workers actually took a look at their "paychecks." The checks were suspiciously small, and bizarre: Quyen received a check for *minus* $4.80. In another infuriating act of audacity, Lee had taken out money for "room and board" from the workers' paychecks—in blatant violation of the signed employment contracts.

Life on Tutuila fell into routines. It was mostly pleasant but frequently infuriating. I realized how intolerant I was and how I did not get this Samoan culture. I disagreed with so much about it. I just did not understand how truth could be malleable. Or how loyalty was encouraged over truth. It seemed to me truth was something that hovered above us all and was what it was and could not be changed by whose blood ran through one's veins. I was not able to communicate in a way that was not direct, and Samoan is not a culture that necessarily appreciates directness (and especially from a mouthy female non-Samoan).

The island of Tutuila is approximately seventeen miles long and five miles wide. The majority of the island has steep mountains that reach up to some two thousand feet above sea level and are covered with lush vegetation. Banana plantations are everywhere, growing strawberry-flavored finger bananas. Taamu leaves are so big they can be worn as Peter Pan hats. Wild orchids are tucked into the jungle growth. Waterfalls are hidden in the mountains. Red and pink and white hibiscus can be put behind one's ear. Huge plumeria trees smell so sweet they cause immediate sadness. Long red ginger blossoms are put next to the bathroom sink and used as soap.

The island is ringed by flatlands in varying widths. In some places, like Tafuna, the flatlands extend a mile or two inland. Some villages are much narrower and the ocean meets the road and the houses on the other side are snuggled up against the mountains. One main road goes (mostly) around the island, although there are many smaller roads that go inland and up the mountains. The bigger roads are paved but most of the secondary ones are not. It is a twisty trip around Tutuila because the road follows the ocean and the bays. Pago Pago Harbor is considered one of the most protected deep-water anchorages west of Hawaii; it cuts several miles into the island and offers boats shelter from most winds.

Governor Tauese Sunia gave a speech stating that economic times in the territory were booming. One of the factors he cited to was the increasing number of cars and trucks on the island (twice as many as last year). In 1989, there were forty-seven hundred vehicles on-island. In 1992 (after hurricanes Ofa and Val) there were fifty-five hundred. This year there were sixty-two hundred.

—*Samoa News,* November 25, 1996

Driving a vehicle on Tutuila could be a singular experience. Drivers are friendly and will invariably stop and let pedestrians cross but will swerve wildly out of their way to take out a dog. Some dogs on Tutuila have the fatalistic habit of stretching out, supine, in the gutter of the main road, where the asphalt is warm. While this does have dire consequences for the hapless dogs, damages are mitigated by the fact that the maximum speed limit on the island is twenty-five miles per hour (except for one stretch of road out by the airport, which is thirty-five).

To say there are a lot of cars and trucks and busses on Tutuila is an understatement. Most extended families have at least one car. The public transportation system is made up of *aiga* busses. Aiga means "family." An aiga bus starts with a small Toyota or Nissan truck frame. Then the cab and end are taken off and a structure approximating a bus is appended onto the former truck frame. It is just like a regular bus, only much smaller. The busses usually have four or five rows of benches and windows all around.

It was the aiga bus decorations that really got my attention, though. They are festooned with all manner of ornamentation and glitz. Some had elaborate scenes air-brushed onto the sides and back; scenes depicting tropical beaches and families and names of villages. The insides were all customized differently. I preferred the ones with cushions on the seats instead of the hard wooden benches, needless to say. There were strings of little decorative puffballs over the windows, posters of Bruce Lee, maps of the island group done in velvet, and calendar wall scrolls from local restaurants. Almost all had a radio that played our local station, KSBS, at decibel levels guaranteed to make me feel a thumping bass line in my collarbone for the next two hours.

The roads were thus busy with (albeit, slow-moving) vehicles most of the time. Driving was often a social event. Local girls would ride in the back of pickup trucks with their long, dark, beautiful hair hanging down over the tailgate. Clearly they had never heard of Isadora Duncan, the modern dancer whose trademark lengthy scarf caught in her roadster wheels and strangled her to death.

It was hard to walk anywhere. Rob liked to walk and did so frequently, especially before we had a car. Tafi and Tua called him "The Walking Man." He was constantly stopped by drivers: cops, clients, friends, congressional candidates, and asked if he needed a ride. The sight of a person actually walking apparently seemed appalling. Some drivers even offered to turn around and travel in the other direction to give him a ride.

We lived one bay and two villages from our office. My problem with walking was being chased by dogs. Clearly a theme. I love dogs but dislike nasty dog encounters. When I got chased by a dog in one of the villages, I would dash into the nearest bush (village) store and hide. Running into Pae'ai's bush store in Fagatogo evoked the biggest reaction. Pae'ai herself would come out and kick the dog in the head, something she told me I should be learning to do for myself at this age.

Locals did have a particular relationship with the road. Although they eschewed walking on it to get somewhere, groups of them routinely stood by the side of the road asking for money from passing drivers. Perhaps because the speed limit is so low, there is more time to hop out of the way of an oncoming vehicle. Thus, church and social and other fund-raising groups (i.e., everyone) stand on the side of the road and beg. They *siva* (dance) in large crowds to attract donations. They have tents set up with fellow fund-raisers sitting at tables with microphones and huge speakers. They accost a person *by name* when one is unfortunate enough to drive by. You are thus called out by your entire given Christian name, blared by microphone into the nearby village, and are chastised to give them money.

The dancers want you to throw dollars at them. They wave the dollars that they have received to invite more. Drivers do in fact toss dollars out of the vehicle windows at them, where they blow around all over the road. The dancers then dart into passing traffic to collect the dollars. This makes for a colorful, fast-moving display, tinged enticingly with the imminent threat of physical injury and doom.

Feeling the need for change, I decided that since my hair was turning silver I would spark things up a bit and dye it. I enlisted Rob's help and we decided to see if blondes had more fun. My hair came out a wan brown in normal light but appeared decidedly pink under the florescent lights in the district courtroom. The following month I ditched the "Hello, Kitty" look and we tried L'Oreal Dark Medium Brown. Because I'm worth it.

"Males with long hair and unmarried couples living together will no longer be allowed to live in Onenoa Village, according to the new set of 'Sa' laws issued by the Onenoa Village Council. [From] 6:45 to 7:00 p.m.—no one is allowed to travel within the village. [There is a] 10:00 p.m. overall curfew. No parties with alcoholic beverages allowed at any time. Loud clapping is prohibited at all times. Yelling or fighting is prohibited at all times. No male is allowed to have long hair. Swimming is prohibited on Sundays, as is doing laundry, except between the hours of 6:00 and 9:15 p.m."

—*Samoa News,* March 3, 1996

In the late 1990s, the sailing *alia Mana O Samoa* made the news. An *alia* is a catamaran. This one was beautiful, built on-island, in the style of the vessels that traversed the South Pacific centuries before. It was hoped it would make the upwind trip to Hawaii. However, this was not to be.

The *Mana O Samoa* was destroyed when the crane that was trying to launch it (from a steep bank) toppled over and crushed the alia where it sat in shallow water in Pago Pago Harbor. Blame was placed, alternatively, on the name, the day of the launching (Sunday), the crane operator (not the regular one because the regular one was in church; this one was a Seventh Day Adventist and had been to church the day before). Several weeks later the alia (repaired and renamed) went into the water without incident. This involved a lot of time, opinions, and beer. The alia bobbed about on the gentle tides ("Passed Water Float Test," said the *Samoa News*) and was readied for her maiden voyage across Pago Pago Harbor. The huge tanbark sail (which sail makers had said all along was too big) was hoisted. The alia and her alarmed crew sprang away from her mooring and zoomed headlong across the harbor. The crew got scared at the amount of sail aloft and pulled it down; they were afraid that they might tip over. The maiden voyage ended with a test tow and more beer.

The island built a brand-new library about this time. It was a big open structure that was actually open most of the time, unlike the old one. The old library, built circa 1940, was located in Fagagogo on a teeny piece of land next to the harbor. It had the usual louvered windows and dark, musty interior. We tried to visit it several times but only got inside once: it was generally locked and maintained no discernible regular hours. I never saw another person utilize it. The one time we actually were allowed inside, we were met by a querulous woman in her fifties who seemed suspicious of our motives. She followed us around the small building and told us not to touch anything.

With the new library, we got a new palagi librarian, straight from the mainland, one with an actual degree in library science. She arrived on Tutuila, excited and nervous about her new position. One of her first tasks, it appeared, was to petition the Fono to release certain funds for books that had been allocated to the library.

So our new librarian nervously prepared half the night before her presentation to the Fono. She brushed up on the background of the public library in general and was prepared to explain her plans for the local library's anticipated growth and outreach programs. She dressed in a traditional *puletasi* for this important occasion. When she arrived to address the stately body, the *matai* introduced her, spoke in Samoan for twenty minutes (the librarian spoke only English and Spanish), and asked her if she had anything to add. She stood before the body of lawmakers, gave her spiel (the money had already been appropriated and the island needed more books and so forth), and the lawmakers conversed some more in Samoan.

They finally rose and a *matai* asked her if they could ask her one question. She acquiesced, anticipating more inquiry on the library's strategy. The question was, "Are you single?"

During this time I had taken to staying up late at night working. I sat in the back room of the little yellow house, at the desk Rob built for me, under the louvered windows that looked over the backyard and the ocean below. Janey and Zuzu were little enough then to curl up in the louvers (although Zuzu would occasionally get stuck when they folded in on her). At night I stared out at the water and imagined all manner of *aitus* (ghosts) gazing back at me through the louvers. Once I thought I heard Hertrudes out in the yard, in the banana plantation. She was yelling at me to go home. Wherever the Sam Hill that was.

Christa, Rob, and I were getting calls from the workers, at night, on a regular basis. Apparently, when the workers entered the compound and came through the manned security gate, the Samoan guards would routinely slap and harass them. One warm night at about eleven o'clock a frightened worker called us to the compound. We arrived and saw our clients inside the fence, crowded together. The guards had punched several workers when they came in earlier and our clients were panicky and sounded desperate. They stood in clumps and gripped the little diagonals in the chain-link fence. Christa was already there and was talking to a group of workers, her hands through the fence and her fingers touching theirs.

"Robert!" I recognized Tam's voice. We hurried over to where she stood, with Quyen and Taller Thuy. "Can you help us get out?" she asked. "We'll try," Rob replied. Just how, I wondered. Clearly we needed to get *into* the compound and meet with our clients and find out what was going on.

Christa and Rob and I tried to get inside through the security gate. We were thwarted by several large Samoan police officers who stood, arms folded, in front of the gate. We stood outside the fence and argued with the police, a fruitless endeavor. We kept saying that we needed to meet with our clients, and they kept not letting us. They said that Lee had to give permission for us to get in and he wasn't there so we couldn't. We were unaccustomed to such a blatant lack of respect for the sixth amendment. (*That* legal argument fell right on deaf ears.) The workers watched us fail and fail. Some looked like they were losing faith in us. No kidding; *I* was losing faith in us. We kept arguing with the police, becoming more frustrated and shrill. The police and the Samoan managers just watched and smoked and laughed. The world was slipping again.

We finally realized we were getting nowhere, slowly. We had to work in a few hours. Christa, Rob, and I crowded close to the fence so we could reassure our clients and promised we'd see them tomorrow. I looked back as Rob drove us away. The compound was dark and the light from the streetlamp reflected on their hundreds of fingers, still clutching the chain-link fence.

CHAPTER SEVEN—NOT
WAVING BUT DROWNING

Lee's minions now regularly patrolled the barbed-wire boundaries and continued to restrict the workers from leaving or meeting with anyone outside the compound. We filed a motion for injunctive relief, which included taking action against the hideously overcrowded living situation; restrictions of freedoms of speech, movement, and association; and the withholding of passports and identification cards. Lee also expelled the four pregnant workers from the factory.

At the hearing on that motion for injunctive relief, we needed certain testimony from Weepy Thu, one of the workers. She had personally witnessed an incident at the factory that could incriminate Lee. Lee had threatened her with immediate deportation, in violation of the existing restrictions against that. No one else had witnessed that threat, just Weepy Thu.

Weepy Thu got her name as she was easily upset and tended toward tears. Christa and I had no idea how she would be when called to testify in court, and we were concerned that she might have a come-apart right on the stand. We talked with her at length about the importance of her testimony and she said over and over that she understood and wanted to testify. But speaking out against one's employer under oath in a public courtroom was far different from telling us in the safety of our office.

On my way to the courthouse I glimpsed Hertrudes hunched by some foliage in the center of the village, doing her endless weeding. A group of local high school girls passed by within inches of her; Hertrudes was invisible to them. The girls, however, were not invisible to Hertrudes. She watched as the girls glided by, all grace and teenaged impunity and long, flowing, dark hair. Her face looked fleetingly wistful and I saw her reach up and smooth her own disheveled silver hair. Then her face turned disdainful again, and she went back to her weeding.

It is important to remember at this point that the workers were largely restricted from leaving the compound on their own. Christa and I communicated regularly with Lee's attorneys and tried repeatedly to prevail on them to allow the workers their freedom. Occasionally, the workers would be allowed out of the compound, and then Lee would capriciously forbid their egress once again. We knew this because Christa, Rob, and I talked with the workers, many of them, each day. They were prisoners.

On the day of the hearing, Lee and his underlings were indeed present in the courtroom. Weepy Thu took the witness stand but kept her head lowered submissively—she was clearly terrified. We went through our preliminary, foundational testimony and she seemed right on track. We brought her testimony around to the information we needed for our case. When I finally asked her the relevant question, she didn't answer. I stood up and asked her again, more softly. She looked at me and silently pleaded with me to stop. I didn't; I couldn't. She finally stood up and her eyes searched the crowded courtroom for someone. At last her eyes found and rested on Comrade Minh, one of the more powerful minions. She took a deep breath, addressed Minh, and tearfully asked, "May I answer the question, please?" Her voice possessed a breathless quality of resigned despair shot with a spark of hope. The courtroom was dead silent and even the judges looked appalled and uncomfortable.

Minh replied in Vietnamese, "You can, but we will see, later."

Thu looked out the window with an expression of anguish. She cleared her throat, looked directly at me, and flatly stated the testimony that we needed. The workers in the courtroom all but applauded, but Minh just glared. We won that hearing.

Rob and I took a brief vacation to the US mainland to see our families in August 2000. That would teach us. During our absence, Lee attempted to deport thirty-eight of the most vocal Vietnamese workers. He called them "troublemakers and agitators." Christa received calls from the workers from the airport as Lee was trying to get them on the plane. We requested yet another show cause and injunctive motion hearing and were able to stay his illegal efforts, but it was wearing (and expensive) on us all. We were sick and tired of riding (unsuccessful) herd on Lee. Life went on.

THIRTY-EIGHT VIETNAMESE WORKERS GO TO COURT FOR ANSWERS
Thirty-eight of Daewoosa Samoa's Vietnamese workers filed a motion against their employer and contractor in

the High Court late yesterday afternoon to seek answers to their possible loss of sponsorship, which may lead to immediate deportation.

The workers want an expedited "show-cause" hearing for Daewoosa to explain why it should not be charged with contempt of court over possible violations of a preliminary injunction that the High Court had issued last December.

Issued and signed by Associate Justice Lyle Richmond, the injunction is to prevent Daewoosa from disturbing or sending any of its Vietnamese workers home or off-island without court approval.

This injunction also bars Daewoosa from ending its sponsorship of the thirty-eight workers without an immigration board hearing and without consulting the law office of Virginia Sudbury, who has been representing the Vietnamese workers for almost a year.

Sudbury is off-island and the matter is being handled by her law practice partner, Christa Lin.

—*Samoa News*, August 17, 2000

On the work front, we applied for and received another federal grant to expand U'una'i Legal Services and now could represent the Vietnamese workers under that grant. We hired two stateside attorneys and moved into a large, and by Samoan standards fancy, office suite. We painted my office purple.

Hang had her babies—twin boys. After the three of them left the hospital, they lived at the compound and had hundreds of mothers.

Our meetings with the workers had become more frequent. We had certified the class, received class action status, and needed to prepare for trial. We were also concerned that if any of the workers *should* be deported prior to trial, we wanted to make provisions to preserve their testimony for trial.

This preservation was easier said than done. We purchased an inexpensive video camera and went about the business of videotaping depositions of the workers. As there were almost three hundred of them this was somewhat daunting. We enlisted the assistance of all U'una'i's lawyers and legal assistants and interviewed each worker, videotaped and under oath, about the specifics of her or his experience with Daewoosa, wage history, and precise amounts owed under the contracts, and the living and nutrition conditions.

Nguyen Thi Nga was our lead and named plaintiff. She and Dung were closely matched after Dung left the compound to live with Dale and Adeline. They were both smarties and picked up English remarkably fast. We had been using Dung as our translator for motion hearings and both women as translators for our meetings with the workers. She was a necessary part of our world and the case and possessed an even-tempered credibility with the workers.

Dung was in an unenviable position, though. Her family in Vietnam had all but disowned her; they were upset that she had gone the way of "agitators and troublemakers" and considered their standing in the community greatly harmed. She was stuck in the territory of American Samoa; she could not legally enter the United States and could be in grave danger should she return to Vietnam. Adeline continued her attempts to obtain her entry into the United States, but thus far had no joy. Dung had left the Daewoosa compound almost a year earlier and chose not to join the lawsuit. Her path through this period of her life was unclear and confusing and she was clearly frustrated.

The last time I saw Dung was in the lobby of the Rainmaker Hotel in mid-August of 2000. We sat on a couch in the run-down room. She was fussing to move about and wanted off the island. Sitting next to her felt like being around a high school senior; she was so elsewhere and distracted. Her world was too small for her and she was coming through the seams. She had fabulous plans. Her excellent English would get her jobs. She wanted to go to Apia and maybe then to Australia or New Zealand. She still began almost every sentence with, "You know ..."

Nga's rosebud light was softer and more consistent. She saw humor easily and had a wistful, expectant way about her. We chose her to be our lead plaintiff after much consideration: it was a public position of vulnerability. She carried a great deal of common sense and kept close counsel with her good friends Tam and Quyen. Nga had been involved in every hearing and knew the points of the case better than most of the workers. Her English was almost as good as Dung's, although she did not believe that herself.

We tried to involve her (and Tam, Quyen, Hung, and a few others) in the strategy of the case whenever we could. They came from a culture that punished singular thought, let alone rebellious action. My legal career was formatted on tenets found in *To Kill a Mockingbird* and I honestly believed any travesty lay in not pursuing one's legal and civil rights. They saw the lawsuit as a potentially life-threatening, radical action. They also viewed its finality in a different way: I saw it in terms of a legal and moral victory and they saw it as representing the hope of resuming normalcy in their lives. I got to walk away; they got to live the results.

There is a place on the island called Sliding Rock. It is located on a beautiful, rocky shore inside the reef. Only a few feet from shore, it has protected tide pools deep enough in some places to swim but shallow enough in others to just sit and enjoy the surrounding beauty. A person could languish for hours in those safe warm pools and watch the churning ocean water outside the reefs. The shore at Sliding Rock is ringed with tall palm trees. It is a quintessential tropical setting.

On a hot Sunday in August, Nga and Dung and some friends went to the beach at Sliding Rock. They went after a storm because that is when it is time to visit the ocean. The tide pools would be filled with unexpected treasures flushed in with the storm's earlier fury. They were sitting in a tide pool, inside the reef, when a big wave unexpectedly rushed over the walls of the tide pool and swept them both out to the still-churning open sea. They were dragged over the shallow reef "like little kittens," as one observer put it. Two experienced surfers and seamen, also visiting the ocean on that day, saw one of the women look to shore and hold up a small hand, waving or drowning.

The eyewitness accounts differ as to what exactly happened next. The friends of Nga and Dung called the police, but when they arrived they lacked the proper sea-going vessels with which to save the women. Several surfers and observers tried to help rescue the women but were unable to do so in the roiling waters outside the tide pools. The stricken crowd watched as Nga and Dung floated away. Their bodies were never recovered and they were presumed drowned.

Their deaths were impossibly shocking. The two women had been instrumental forces in and stalwart faces of this frightening lawsuit. The workers were devastated by the deaths of Dung and Nga. Their already-low morale plummeted. There was rampant speculation that somehow their deaths were the result of nefarious means; but there is no evidence of that nor do I believe it. I think it was a hideous, tragic accident that was just that, and all that encompasses.

A few days later we held a memorial service for Nga and Dung at the Jones's house in Pago Pago. Most of the workers attended, along with scores of locals and friends. I imagined that Dale, Dung, and Nga would hear our words of remembrance and give us tenacity and succor. As we drove the winding road around the island and along the ocean to the Jones's house, I confidently informed Robbie that I just would not cry *one little bit* at the memorial service and would (for once) comport myself with stately grace and dignity. I would provide a calm and steely inspiration to the workers and give them strength through my remarkable composure.

I stepped out of our car, saw Tam, burst into tears, and finally stopped when I went to bed some twelve hours later. I cried mightily through all eulogies, including the one I gave. I cried through trips to the bathroom and the buffet table and during grace. I cried through dinner and through laughing at jokes and funny stories about Dung and Nga. I cried driving home with Robbie and when we got home to our kitties Janey and Zuzu. I am even crying as I write this now, many years later; and that is the tenacity of love.

TWO VIETNAMESE WOMEN SWEPT INTO SEA, FEARED DEAD

Two Vietnamese women are presumed dead after being swept out to sea Sunday afternoon at the Sliding Rock area in Vailoatai, although a search is still underway today to locate their bodies, the commissioner of public safety's office confirmed to *Samoa News*.

An eyewitness to the tragedy, Rev. Rob Stip of the

sponsor of the workers, Kil-Soo Lee, wasn't paying them, this made no sense.) Nonetheless, the ASG decided that it needed to step in and prevent these workers from this moonlighting. Public sentiment was shifting to follow the anti-Vietnamese, anti-U'una'i, and anti-us stance taken by the American Samoa government.

Kil-Soo Lee tried again to fire the three pregnant workers and deport them back to Vietnam. We fought it in court and won, again; but it was hollow and to our clients, seemed to change nothing.

COURT: DAEWOOSA SAMOA CANNOT FIRE PREGNANT WORKERS

Daewoosa Samoa has again felt the wrath of the High Court of American Samoa.

The High Court ruled on Monday that the garment factory cannot terminate the employment of three pregnant workers and return them to Vietnam.

Instead, the court added, these workers are to be put back to work "with pay, retroactively from October 2, 2000." The court also found Daewoosa Samoa and its management in contempt of court for their violations of several court orders.

"In light of defendants' constant failure to heed this court's orders, and the nondeterring effect of previously imposed sanction, it appears that we must resort to the severe penalty of imprisonment and more substantial fines before defendants will begin to take the court's orders seriously," noted the ruling.

The court then sentenced Daewoosa owner-president Kil-Soo Lee to jail for ten days. Lee and Daewoosa were also each fined $10,000.

—Samoa News, October 25, 2000

DAEWOOSA SAMOA'S FATE IS UP TO THE HIGH COURT

What is the administration doing about Daewoosa Samoa workers roaming the streets?

Governor Tauese Sunia said the final decision on that controversial issue rests with the High Court, which must still hear a class-action suit brought on by Daewoosa's workers against Daewoosa.

He noted that the court also has an injunction against the company that prevents the workers from being deported at the company's discretion without court approval and or a review by the workers attorney Virginia Sudbury.

—Samoa News, October 30, 2000

I was devastated. I thought we were doing the right thing in representing the Vietnamese workers, that they were in dire straits and any sound and rational person (or government) would rush to our assistance—or at the very least not impede our efforts. Instead, we were treated as if we, and our clients, had violated the law. I then realized we were truly going this alone.

I found a lump in my breast. I had little reason to have faith in the medical care provided in American Samoa, but I needed a biopsy and had one at the LBJ Tropical Medical Center. I had to wait for the results—it had to be mailed off-island for an accurate reading. Three weeks later I found out that it was mercifully benign, but those weeks took months to pass.

The workers, weary of the struggle and exhausted from the emotions of the past weeks, discussed returning to Vietnam. They told us that even *that* fate might be preferable to remaining in American Samoa in this wretched state.

Chapter Eight—It's Chinatown, Jake

November 28, 2000, was a Tuesday. I remember waking up that morning and thinking I had no court appearances, and the glorious tropical day stretched out before me. I thought I could get much accomplished at the office that day without having to go to court. By the time the day ended and we finally went to bed early the next morning, it would be a black Tuesday indeed.

That morning Rob and I left the little yellow house and drove down the mountain to the U'una'i office, through the villages along the ocean. We saw Hertrudes weeding under the trees across from the High Court. She was wearing a cardboard box on her head and looked grim, as usual.

The entire U'una'i office was gearing up in preparation for trial, set to begin in six weeks. Things had been mercifully quiet at the Daewoosa factory for the past week or so, and we hoped Lee had decided to stop his almost-constant harassment and imprisonment of our clients. The workers were still in a state of numb grief since Nga and Dung had drowned. Their tenacity was present but their will seemed cracked.

It was a rare day when we didn't hear from at least a dozen of our clients; several of them had cell phones. That morning, right after I got to my desk, Grace buzzed me from the outer office with the message that Tam was on the phone and something was not right—she sounded frantic. I picked up the telephone and could barely hear Tam's voice over the cries and shrieks around her. It sounded like she was standing in the middle of a riot.

"Virginia!" she began, in an urgent voice. Tam's voice generally had a calming manner about it but now it sounded thinner, and higher. "Come now, please, to the factory." She paused. "They are beating us."

The words were all the more chilling because of the composed way she conveyed them. I looked at Rob's questioning face, and for one second everything got very small and clear and poignant, like in a glass paperweight.

Christa arrived at the office in time to see me switch the telephone to speaker and motion for Rob to grab the car keys. Piped out through the speakerphone, the cries at the factory sounded much louder and more insistent. Tam's voice continued with requests that we come, immediately, please. *Now.*

I stayed at the office while Christa and Rob jumped in the car and sped to the compound. I told Tam we would keep her on the speakerphone until they arrived. Grace and I tried to keep her calm. Because of the way the phone system was wired Tam's voice and the horrific background melee were piped through our entire office. Everyone in the office was transfixed—staff and clients and lawyers alike.

I listened to Tam describe what she was seeing and imagined her wandering in the midst of the fracas, cell phone to her ear, relaying what she saw. She kept saying there was blood everywhere, in bits and scratches. I didn't understand then but later it made sense—this was a garment factory, and the cuts were made by scores of tiny sharp sewing scissors. I asked who was wielding them. *Who is beating you?*

The Samoans, Tam replied. She sounded almost weary. The Vietnamese workers had been sewing and had run out of material. Running out of material was a big deal at a garment factory. It means that no one sews and no garments are made and no money comes in.

The main working floor of the garment factory was huge—about ten thousand square feet. A partial second floor housed Lee's offices. Those offices stretched the width of the factory and were equipped with windows, so Lee and his minions could watch the sewing activity on the factory floor below. The lack of material was critical, and by all accounts Kil-Soo Lee was angry about the delays this would cause. I imagine he must have been in a particularly ugly mood that day, because why else would he order what he had? I also suppose at that time I still thought him to possess a shred of humanity.

On November 28 the factory was quickly running out of material. Kil-Soo Lee could look out his watchtower windows and see the piles of material next to each worker grow small and then disappear. He could see the workers relaxing idly as they had more free time. He could see, as a worker ran out of sewing, she would stretch and leave her machine and wander about, maybe for a smoke outside or to chat up her friends a few tables away. Workers lolled across the tables and their machines, talking and laughing with their friends. The attitude in the factory was party-like—like when school is unexpectedly let out early.

It is important to note that the Daewoosa factory also employed thirty or so Samoan workers. These workers did not sew; instead, they worked in the packing department and loaded the heavy boxes of materials, supplies, and equipment necessary to run the factory. They all knew each other and had an apartness from the Vietnamese and the Chinese workers. There was very little mixing. Nu'uuli, the Samoan floor manager, probably interacted with the workers more than most as he patrolled the floor and made sure production continued.

This day was especially vexing. Kil-Soo Lee was angry because of the lack of material, and the workers were cheeky. From the floor, Nu'uli could see his boss pace back and forth in this upper offices, flinging his arms around as he yelled into his cell phone. Finally Lee hung up and peered into the factory below. He spotted Nu'uuli and motioned for him to come up to his offices.

Nu'uuli knew that Lee was already annoyed about the slow rate of production. Maybe because of the sudden deaths of Dung and Nga, maybe because the workers hadn't been getting paid, maybe because of the lawsuit—production had been slipping. Several weeks ago Lee had reminded Nu'uuli of important upcoming shipment deadlines and told Nu'uuli he would receive a raise when the containers were shipped.

But November 28 was a different day. Nu'uuli trooped up the long wooden stairway to Lee's offices. "Production is too slow already!" Lee shouted at Nu'uuli as he came into the room. "It is the fault of the Vietnamese—tell the Samoans to beat any Vietnamese who are not working; if anyone dies, I will take responsibility!"

Nu'uuli dutifully returned to the packing department and repeated these appalling words to the Samoan workers. For added incentive he also related that Lee had said that if deadlines were missed, the Samoans would not receive *their* paychecks.

Nu'uuli then returned to confront the idle Vietnamese workers. He stood near the front of the factory and told them in a commanding voice to get back to work, and right now. He stood next to Quyen, who sat cross-legged on the table next to her machine. Quyen told him again there were no materials upon which to sew. According to some accounts, she thoughtfully added a somewhat florid description of just what he could do with his orders. This sass was just enough to get Nu'uuli ripped. He reached out and grabbed Quyen by her hair and yanked her toward him. The Samoan workers—watching what happened and primed by the words of Lee—rushed out of the packing department and onto the factory floor. They were armed with scissors, sticks, and pipes. The Samoans brutally attacked the smaller Asian workers.

Nu'uuli called a female security guard for assistance and began to pull Quyen toward the front of the factory. As he was pulling Quyen, a worker knocked Nu'uuli to the floor. They tussled, and Nu'uuli lost his grip on Quyen, who slipped away into the growing brawl. Nu'uuli straddled the worker and punched him repeatedly. Finally the worker squirmed out of Nu'uuli's arms and ran away, with Nu'uuli fast after him to continue the beating.

Despite the fact that someone yelled that the police were coming, a Samoan security guard grabbed and held Quyen while another Samoan woman named Sialava'a Fagaima moved toward the front factory door. She punched Quyen repeatedly while Quyen was being dragged. Fagaima grabbed a sharpened PVC pipe and thrust it, using both hands, into Quyen's left eye. Quyen's eye was sliced in half.

That is when Tam called us. Workers were running about and screaming, trying to evade the armed Samoans. Another Vietnamese worker who was pummeled by the Samoans suffered the partial loss of his hearing. Many of our other clients suffered injuries, thankfully mostly minor. But blood was everywhere—on the floor, on the machines, and on the workers. Most escaped back to their barracks, where they huddled together in relative, if temporary, safety.

When Nu'uuli returned and reached the front door of the factory, Quyen was leaning against the wall, holding a bloody cloth over her eye. The remaining workers were weeping, bunched together between the long sewing tables. Nu'uuli stood near the open door way, legs astride and arms folded. He repeatedly chanted to the stunned workers, over and over: "This is what you want?" In perfect matched time, as with an answering cheer at a rugby game, the female Samoan standing next to him regularly slammed her pipe into the floor while chanting, "This is what you get."

It took Rob and Christa no more than seven minutes to get to the factory compound, but to me it seemed an hour. I stayed in my office, called the police, imagined what legal action we would take, started drafting a motion for injunctive relief (who knew for what specifically but that could come later), and generally fretted. I left the speakerphone on, and Tam's breathing and the cries around her eventually became part of the background, like some macabre soundscape. I was fascinated by my powerlessness, by what I could not do. Then I heard the strong and capable voices of Rob and Christa embrace Tam and the others, and then the phones went dead.

I closed the offices and went to meet Rob and Christa and the workers. We finally found Quyen—unbelievably, instead of being taken to the hospital, she and the other injured workers were arrested by the police and taken to the Tafuna Correctional Facility. When the ambulance finally arrived at the correctional facility, the workers were sitting at a table outside in the sun, surrounded by Samoan prison guards. Quyen was bleeding badly from her eye and was woozy and confused. The ambulance took Quyen and the other workers to the LBJ Tropical Medical Center. Many hours later, in the wee hours of the next day, we would learn that Quyen's eye had been irreparably damaged and would have to be removed.

Now here is a bizarre yet heartening note about Quyen's eye. Remember: the LBJ Tropical Medical Center was not known far and wide for its advanced medical treatment. In fact, as has been mentioned, it was consistently on the short list of where not to go when sick. It did, however, receive the generous and frequent benefit of visiting physicians, who specialized in certain areas. Incredibly, that very afternoon, a doctor named Dr. Whitehouse, an ophthalmologist, landed in Pago Pago for a three-day stint at LBJ.

We waited at the hospital while Dr. Whitehouse operated on Quyen that night for many hours. We were told that if he was not successful in removing what shreds were left of her left eye, the infection would quickly spread into her other eye and she would lose that eye as well. He was successful and saved Quyen's right eye. He is our hero. I have never met Dr. Whitehouse, although I would certainly like to do so to tell him that myself.

WORKER LOSES EYE IN
DAEWOOSA SAMOA MELEE

A melee broke out early yesterday morning among the Samoan and foreign workers at the Daewoosa Samoa garment factory in Tafuna.

A Vietnamese woman, identified as Miss Quyen, eventually lost her left eye that had been seriously damaged in the fight, despite a valiant surgical effort at the LMJ Tropical Medical Authority to save it. At least a dozen other workers suffered minor injuries.

"These workers are terrified to go back to work and they don't feel safe and protected," [the worker's lawyer Virginia Sudbury] stated, noting that she has informed her clients not to return to work today.

Samoa News has learned that many of the workers have stayed away from the Daewoosa compound and are instead being "hosted" in local homes throughout the community.

—*Samoa News*, November 29, 2000

The next day Nu'uuli and Virginia Solia'i, another Samoan manager, met with the Samoan workers. Solia'i handed out forms to Samoan workers and instructed them to record what had happened the previous day at the factory. She told the workers that the forms were for the police and they should be filled out and returned to her. She instructed the Samoan workers to say that Sialava'a Fagaima had not gouged out Quyen's eye, and to state that the Vietnamese had started the incident by rushing the Samoans with scissors and poles. Nu'uuli and the Samoan workers agreed with this falsified course of conduct, and each dutifully wrote down the version of the melee that Virginia Solia'i told them to. But we would not know this until many years later.

We contacted the local attorney general about imposing criminal charges against the Samoans and Lee for the riot, but the American Samoa government steadfastly refused to press any charges, despite the numerous statements filed by the workers. They said that because of the statements written by the Samoans, there was not sufficient evidence to prosecute anyone.

After filing our extensive but apparently ineffectual police reports, Christa, Rob, and I went back to the factory. Unbelievably, we were again denied entry to the compound. The frightened workers were again forbidden to leave, and there was much weeping and shrieking and clawing at the barbed-wire fence that separated us. The Samoan police once again guarded the gate and would not let us through to see our clients.

We knew the workers were hungry and felt hopeless about their situation. They received growing pressure from their families to drop the lawsuit, to avoid dangerous political repercussions against the entire clan in Vietnam. The twists in the case fascinated the island population, and the *Samoa News* ran the front-page teaser, "See page 3 for your daily dose of Daewoosa."

We all faced a constant barrage of derision and hostility. The workers were disheartened and terrified and wanted nothing more than to go back to their families and the relative safety—and anonymity—of Vietnam. Christa and I understood their feelings and were prepared to continue with the trial without the physical presence of our clients. We had our video depositions to present instead of their direct testimony. We knew that without the workers themselves, however, the case would be less persuasive and our chances for victory would be lessened. I felt supremely powerless—after all, what could I really offer these workers? Certainly I could not guarantee their safety; I couldn't even keep them intact and *alive*. I had been resoundingly unsuccessful thus far at obtaining their back wages. What business did I have thinking I could make a difference to these workers? The obstacles we faced were overwhelming. I couldn't speak their language and had to rely on stilted, uncertain translations from our clients, who were learning English as the case progressed. We had no idea what we were going to do for translation at trial and could not afford to bring over someone from off-island on our limited resources. I could not support them—Christa, Rob, and I had already put in enormous sums of our own money into the lawsuit.

Lee, on the other hand, appeared to enjoy a seemingly endless supply of capital, in addition to the tacit support of the American Samoan government. His prosperous lifestyle changed not at all, and the numerous citations for contempt against him did not alter his treatment of our clients. If anything, he became more audacious and acted with even greater impunity. The workers became more and more depressed. They were not even receiving adequate food and were losing weight; several had stopped menstruating due to weight loss. They thought there was no other option but to return to Vietnam and face the shame and humiliation of their families—reputations be damned.

Christa, Rob, and I privately discussed sending the workers home to Vietnam. I really didn't want to. We realized, however, that there was no work for them outside the nonpaying Daewoosa factory where they were currently virtually imprisoned. They were far from their disappointed families and aliens here in the territory. It was grim all around.

We finally agreed with the wishes of the workers and set the matter for hearing. We would ask that the court order Lee to send the workers back to their home countries, mostly Vietnam but also China.

The acrimonious hearing took place in the upstairs courtroom during a flashing, roaring thunderstorm. Justice Richmond's courtroom was constantly illuminated by bright flashes of lightening immediately followed by ripping booms of thunder. The rain fell incessantly, loud on the wooden roof and on the verandas that surrounded the second floor of the courthouse. The courtroom was crowded with workers. Since the riot they clung together and were more somber and watchful. The hearing transpired in English (and Korean) since Dung had drowned and we had no court-approved Vietnamese translator. We presented our evidence and our arguments and asked the court to order Lee to pay for the return of our clients to Vietnam. Our arguments were strong. American Samoan immigration law strictly dictated that when non-American Samoans are brought to the island to work, a bond must be posted equal to the amount of their return ticket home. The court granted our motion.

Christa and I felt bittersweet about the ruling but had resigned ourselves to this being the only realistic way off the island for these workers so they could get on with their lives. There was no way they would be allowed into any of the fifty states, so applying for green cards or other temporary visas was out. They certainly did not want to remain on the tiny island of Tutuila for the rest of their lives, ever separated from their families and culture. They had no choice but to return to their homes. We knew of no other options.

Christa stood up and asked Justice Richmond to give Lee a date certain by which to return the bond money and purchase the airplane tickets to Vietnam and China. Aitofele Sunia, Lee's attorney, asked that we all approach the bench. In hushed tones, he told us the dire news: Lee had no money to pay the workers' transportation home! Apparently, the American Samoan government, ever a friend to Kil-Soo Lee, had *waived* the almost three hundred required bond payments and allowed Kil-Soo Lee to bring the workers in without following the law. Thus, there was no money to pay for their tickets home. Here the workers were, and here they would apparently stay.

Lee left the courtroom smiling at the judges and shaking his attorney's hand. The judges filed silently from the bench, and we were left in the courtroom with the court staff and our workers, who sat watchfully. Adeline and her friend Catherine were there, and Bill and the Concerned Citizens group were present at most hearings. Christa and I frowned down at the counsel table and organized our pleadings and notes. Neither of us knew quite how to break this devastating news to our clients. Our clients stood silently, waiting and watching us closely. Finally, Christa and I turned to them and attempted to relate what had happened. Tam was our informal translator—her English was better than anyone else's but she was still not fluent. She stood in front of me, watched assiduously as I softly related what had happened, and turned and haltingly told the others.

We told them that while we won, technically, they would not be going back to Vietnam anytime soon because Lee had no money. Tam translated these words into Vietnamese. The workers appeared crushed. Tam looked at me searchingly, and I could feel her *willing* me to tell her more words to translate; good words, like they would be paid and go home right away and see their mothers. I was breathless with the power I lacked. One tiny tear trickled down Tam's cheek, and I started to cry. This started the other workers into crying, and Christa, Adeline, and Catherine as well, and before long the room was filled with weeping women, the court staff included.

Several days later we learned that our trial was set to begin January 18, 2001. The workers would be present for the trial—but we didn't know how they would eat, or live, in the meantime. Everything depended on the outcome of the trial—or so we thought.

Governor Sunia, hoping to finally rid the territory of the political embarrassment of the workers' presence, made an enormous tactical blunder. He circumvented the US government and engaged in negotiations directly with the ambassador to Vietnam. These conversations took place without the involvement—or knowledge—of the US government. I imagine that this behavior did not endear him to Washington. He and Congressman Eni Faleomavaega also engaged in a furious game of "pass the worker" and publicly blamed each other. The American Samoa government was called inept, bumbling, and other disparaging terms. But the governor and the congressman continued to blame the workers themselves for their dilemma—and of course Christa, Rob, and me. Clearly, if it wasn't for us taking the case, none of this would have happened.

TAUESE ASKS VIETNAM FOR HELP IN SENDING WORKERS BACK HOME

The American Samoa government has approached the Vietnamese government about paying for the return airfares of their countrymen and women who work for Daewoosa Samoa if the beleaguered company is unable to do so.

The issue was outlined in a letter from Governor Tauese Sunia to the Chargé d' Affairs at the Vietnamese Embassy in Washington, DC. The letter is a formal response to embassy inquiries about the November 28 melee at the Daewoosa factory.

— *Samoa News,* January 19, 2001

One supremely hilarious thing did happen around that time. Kil-Soo Lee's foot got run over by a car. The *Samoa News* initially reported that he had been "seriously injured" in a hit-and-run, but that account turned out to be hasty.

Immediately after the incident, reporting from the LBJ emergency room, Virginia Soli'ai sorrowfully relayed that Lee had been "run down" outside the Daewoosa compound. However, the next day the driver came forward and stated indignantly that it was not a hit-and-run and that she had instead remained on the scene after she ran over his foot.

Apparently, the driver of the car was dropping off some of the workers at the factory. Lee got mad at her and followed her out to her car. He wrote down her license plate number and tried to prevent her from leaving. He yelled that he had called the police. The driver didn't seem to be affected by Lee's antics and started her car and inched it forward. Lee kept shouting and waving and standing in front of the car. Eventually, the inevitable happened and the driver, needing to be elsewhere, drove the only direction she could to get the heck out of there and ran right over Lee's foot. She may not have meant to, but it surely seemed a good thing at the time.

Preparing for a major class-action trial is much like preparing to sail a small boat across the ocean: it consumes you. Nothing can be left to chance, all facts and knowledge and skills must be expertly organized and honed, and there must be a spare set of everything. Our little house in the jungle looked like a war council room—every available flat surface was covered with pleadings and exhibits and notes for the trial. We hadn't eaten a meal at the table in weeks—there was no room and less inclination. The cats no longer slept at the foot of the bed as that was covered with papers too.

In a surprise move, Marie Lafaele, a local attorney, assumed cocounsel status for Lee and Daewoosa with Aitofele Sunia. One of Marie's brothers, Birdsall Ala'ilima, was Governor Sunia's special assistant. Another of her brothers, Charlie, drafted the original Articles of Incorporation and Bylaws for the U'unai'i Legal Services. (He never obtained funding. He gave us those documents in 1997 and encouraged us to try to obtain that backing. We obtained funding from the Violence Against Women Granting Agency to fund U'unai'i in 1998. I am forever grateful to him for doing so.)

We received constant pressure from the American Samoa government about the political implications of our lawsuit. Rob and I were plagued by nightly telephone hang-ups and personal threats. This caused talk and suspicion about our role in this case. As usual, I was too daft to notice the deepening lack of support in public opinion. (My grasp of the subtle yet inability to see the obvious is a reoccurring theme in my life. Once, on a recess in the middle of a divorce hearing several years earlier, I was out on the courthouse veranda. I represented the husband. The wife and three other women came from the parking lot, up the courthouse steps, in my direction. I remember thinking they were coming over to say hey. Just as they got closer, another attorney, a Samoan woman, grabbed me by the neck and escorted me through the doors and into the courthouse lobby. She said they were not coming to say hey. She said they were coming to do me harm and cut off my hair. Go figure.)

It was finally procedurally time to go after the assets of the factory. We filed a motion to appoint a receiver to take over Daewoosa, and the court granted that motion. Control of the factory was finally taken away from Lee, and we all took that as a portentous sign.

Meanwhile, Kil-Soo Lee's lawyer had not complied with our discovery requests for the upcoming trial. Christa and I again brought a motion before the court to compel them to give us the documents and evidence we had previously requested. The court granted our request and told us we could actually go through the compound and search. The court ordered that we should take an FBI agent with us.

The FBI had just recently arrived on-island; they were all very nice to us but assured us that all they could do was investigate, and that would take a long time. The FBI did not come often to the island, although their presence was not unheard of. They always kept a low profile, dressed in aloha shirts, and left in the night. We didn't really recognize the import of the fibbies being there at the time. When we tried to discuss the case with them, they were not terribly encouraging; but we were sure happy to have someone in the federal government listen to our clients. Plus, they brought me pretzels from the mainland.

Up in Lee's Daewoosa office they found all sorts of interesting documents that we would use at trial. They went through Lee's private quarters and found a great big apothecary jar, two or three liters in size, the kind you'd see in an old-time store and that you could put your hand in and take out a whole fistful of candy. The jar was full of white pills shaped like caplets. The apothecary jar was nearly half full. We believe that the pills were Quaaludes.

They kept looking through Lee's bedroom and found videos of questionable taste. Most had an institutional theme and involved young girls, underwear, and discipline.

In early December 2000, representatives from the Vietnamese government flew to the territory and met with ASG officials. This came about because of the vast amount of international publicity that had been paid to the case in the Asian Pacific community. We believed the Vietnamese government was worried about the several hundred of their citizens left in an American territory without the ability to either work or leave. The members of the contingent called each other "comrade."

The Vietnamese contingent was led by a woman named Madam Mai. While she was on-island, Madam Mai met with the workers (without us) and advised them, in the strongest possible terms, on the wisdom of dropping their lawsuit. It will come to no good, she emphasized. She ate with them and stroked their arms and told them that she understood how they missed their mothers. She spent her days with them and won some converts. The workers were only hurting themselves and shaming their families and the Vietnamese government, she reiterated. The lawsuit was all bad, she said. Several workers told us that she also personally threatened them with direct physical harm and told them she had a shotgun. Thus, every time Christa and I mentioned her name in our conversations, we sliced our hands across our necks and made a *hhwwiiick* sound. To this day we still do.

After meeting with the Vietnamese contingent, the ASG governor, Tauese Sunia, issued several public statements. He announced on the (government-owned) radio and television that American Samoa was not to be considered a proper route into the United States. He stated that our clients were forbidden to walk freely around the streets at night. Tauese also said that "... he will talk with the Samoan workers, not only as the governor but as a father and traditional leader to impose the need for better working relationship. The Samoan workers told the *Samoa News* that they and their Vietnamese coworkers have always worked well together—it is the Vietnamese worker's lawyers who are making things worse" (*Samoa News*, December 8, 2000).

News of the riot at the factory swept across the South Pacific and received a great deal of coverage. Congressman Faleomavaega bristled at what he called "misinformation" that gave a negative impression of the territory. "I'm not too happy with some of the reporting," said Faleomavaega. "They are giving the impression that Samoans are beating the Vietnamese."

LOCAL LEADERS CALLED ON TO EXPLAIN DAEWOOSA INCIDENT

Congressman Faleomavaega Eni stated, "As I listen to both the Vietnamese workers' and Samoan workers' version, it's hard to determine who is right."

[The governor] claims that the Vietnamese worker who lost her eye was sleeping on the job, refusing to work, and "once again I guess she worked somewhere else at night" (this is how the governor suggests the women were involved as "tikitiki girls").

"And when the supervisor tried to remove her from the work place, she slapped the supervisor ... which caused the Samoan workers there to join in," he explained. (These statements have been criticized by the Vietnamese workers' attorney, Virginia Sudbury.)

—*Samoa News*, December 18, 2000

It was New Year's Eve. Rob, Christa, and I were hopeful at the prospect of things getting better—or at least resolved—with the coming year. The workers, also invigorated by the powerful auspice of the New Year, invited us all over to the factory compound to celebrate New Year's Eve with them. They had somehow procured food and spices and the use of the factory kitchen. Rob and I, weary of the unremitting intensity of the situation, begged off; but Christa and her friend Joel attended.

They were treated to an exotic, colorful, and heartfelt feast, of which the workers were justifiably proud. The mood was celebratory but ended abruptly when Nu'uuli stormed into the cafeteria and loudly ordered Christa off the compound. She refused to leave and explained that she had the court's permission to be there, but Nu'uuli would not listen and left in an angry snit. The workers were shocked and clearly unsettled at this behavior toward their attorney and spoke to each other in hushed tones. A few minutes later a squad of burly Samoan police officers entered the room and arrested Christa for trespass. As she was forcibly taken to jail, Christa attempted to reassure the workers, but they stood in tight clumps and watched, stricken and silent. The wonderful promises of the holiday evening were dashed. 2001 had arrived.

LAWYER ACCUSED OF TRESPASSING AT DAEWOOSA

Christa Lin, one of the two attorneys representing Daewoosa Samoa's Vietnamese workers, was taken into police custody New Year's Eve for allegedly trespassing into the company's Tafuna compound. However, she was not jailed but was released instead "in the spirit of the holiday," according to Lin's law partner, Virginia Sudbury. "The police first booked Christa and wanted to incarcerate her without bail."

—*Samoa News*, January 2, 2001

CHAPTER NINE—FEELING HEAVEN SLIPPING

In early January 2001, in a bizarre political step, Marie Lafaele, Lee's counsel, filed a motion in the Daewoosa case alleging that the composition of the U'una'i board was improper and attacked the bylaws and thus U'una'i's representation of the workers. Remember: her brother, Charlie Ala'ilima, had written the bylaws many years before.

U'una'i represented the Daewoosa workers in January 2001 under the auspice of the new Health and Humans Services grant on behalf of indigent clients. Prior to that, my private law office had represented them as they did not qualify under our initial VAWA grant.

Marie lost her motion to have us removed as counsel of record. Failing to obtain relief through the courts, she called a meeting of the American Samoa Bar Association to address this issue and my 150 pounds of alleged badness. She sought sanctions against me and badly wanted me off the Daewoosa case—some three weeks prior to trial.

That evening I drove from the office to the meeting, several villages away. I saw Hertrudes. She was wading in shallow water and held her arms outstretched. She appeared to be singing to the ocean. I wondered what scared her, if anything did.

At the time I was the president of the American Samoa Bar Association. The bar meeting on this particular night was gruesome. I remember the meeting was at Rubbles, a local restaurant and bar, and there was some sort of a vote to get me removed as U'una'i director. In the usual enlightened island fashion, the vote was split strictly along racial lines, with the exception of Elvis Patea, who voted with the palagis. I was to remain as director. However, through a hostile takeover, a new U'una'i board was put into place. One of the members was Tautai Aviata Faalevao, the public defender. To say that we did not get along was an understatement. He appeared to hate me, like much of the government seemed to as well. During one painful board meeting, he told me it would be a good day when I left the island.

Unwisely, though, he also went on the local radio station, KSBS, and stated publicly that I had embezzled money from U'una'i. I hopped right on that big fat lie and called another attorney and he made Avi retract the statement the next day. Avi did, thus avoiding being sued into the next century. The board was so hostile to us that at one meeting we placed a tape recorder in plain sight on a desk to record what they were saying. Halfway through they noticed the tape recorder and left in a cluster huff. I still have the tape. The trial in *Nga v. Daewoosa* was to begin in two weeks.

Trial preparation was incessant and unrelieved. Christa and I were on the telephone with each other almost hourly and were as likely to phone the other at 11:00 p.m. as 11:00 a.m. Our conversations did not end, they merely continued. We neatly organized our exhibits into labeled notebooks and memorized several bankers' boxes full of documents. We spent hours with our witnesses, reviewing anticipated testimony. We knew, cold, the number of hours Tam or Taller Thuy or Hang worked and the exact square footage of the workers' barracks and what Quyen was wearing when she was stabbed. We thought we were ready. Our clients were effectively imprisoned at the compound. We filed more statements to support criminal charges, but the police "lost" them and the case was never forwarded for prosecution. Lee again failed to pay the factory's bills, and the electricity at the factory was shut off for several days. In high summer, the tropical Pacific heat and humidity are intense.

Two days before trial Christa and I visited the Daewoosa compound and were unexpectedly allowed in. The workers were agitated and chattering and it appeared that some of them just received money from an unknown source. We climbed the stairs to the upper management office above the factory common and observed Kil-Soo Lee, the Samoan managers, and an unknown Asian man with a briefcase. The workers had told us they had seen the briefcase opened and it was stuffed with US currency. We later saw a briefcase sitting on an empty factory table down below, and wondered what was inside.

Kil-Soo Lee was furious when he discovered that Christa and I were wandering about the factory, unsupervised. The next day he had his lawyer file a request for an emergency restraining order to keep Christa and me off the factory grounds, to prohibit us from talking to the media, and for harassment. The court immediately denied their requests.

One of our most loyal fans was Fisaga, Kathleen's daughter. She was about five years old then and was a beautiful and observant child. Given some of their shared experiences, this was a testament to the steadiness and tenacity of her mother. Fisaga had learned a song in school: "The warriors of God are mighty and strong." But she sang "The lawyers of God are mighty and strong" and Kathleen did not correct her.

DAEWOOSA SHUT DOWN, AWAITS EMERGENCY CASH INFUSION

Daewoosa Samoa was shut down last Thursday by the company's court-appointed receiver, according to newly appointed general manager, Ben Solaita. The shutdown will continue until the company's money situation improves, Solaita added.

"There is no money to operate the company," said Solaita. "And we do not have any predictions on when production will return to normal, pending the receipt of any cash infusion."

—Samoa News, January 18, 2001

DAEWOOSA HAS NO MONEY TO FEED FOREIGN WORKERS

Daewoosa Samoa's Vietnamese workers will finally have their day in court as their long-awaited class-action suit goes to trial this morning in the High Court.

The trial was initially planned to run two days but could extend well into next week, depending on how many workers and other witnesses will be testifying during the trial.

—Samoa News, January 18, 2001

About this time I *really* needed to get off that island. I generally remember my dreams (sometimes too well) and like to think they are helpful and illustrative of where I find myself at the moment. For months before we left the island, I dreamt the same dream over and over: that we would not ever make it back to the mainland, that I would never get off that island, that my life would never change. That the island would cover me. That the plane home would crash, that we would lose the kitties, that I would lose my Robbie, that circumstances would conspire to prevent me from leaving, and that I would have to live there forever. I do not think I can adequately convey the claustrophobia I felt while living on that island. I understand it is a beautiful tropical paradise. I know it had stunning scenery if you looked up. I saw that it was covered with verdant tropical foliage and cool myths and unusual food. I get that the people were, largely, friendly. But if you looked down from the mountains, if you were not Samoan or able to fit in, if you were loud and outspoken and represented unpopular victims of domestic violence and the Daewoosa workers, you were known or visible wherever you went. People pointed at you and asked intrusive questions and were not nice. When you went to the only psychologist at the LBJ hospital because you feared you had lost what little was left of your mind and wanted to save that little piece, and the receptionist said, "Virginia Sudbury? That big lawyer? And now *you're crazy!*," all the while pointing at you so all you could see was her large laughing face and the tip of her finger getting bigger and darker and coming at you like a battering ram. You saw members of the current administration glare at you at the local restaurants on Saturday mornings when you were having breakfast with your husband and you glared back, because by that time all you knew how to do was be angry and fight. You stopped smiling for an entire month before your husband pointed out that he hadn't seen you smile in that long; when you did finally smile it felt weird and fake on your mouth. You hated your life. You hated the territory of American

Virginia Lynn Sudbury

Samoa, the attitudes, the limitedness, the lack of conceptual thought, the imperiousness. You missed your mom and your little sister. You wanted to go home, wherever that was.

CHAPTER TEN—YOUR STORY'S TOUCHING BUT IT SOUNDS LIKE A LIE

January 18, 2001, the morning of the first day of trial, I was as sick as a dog. I had a low-grade fever, a raging headache, a sore lower back, diarrhea, hives on my elbows, eczema in the shape of New Zealand creeping across my forehead, cramps, and, of course, my period. Clearly I was ready to operate at my best. Fortunately, Christa and I arrived at the courtroom early enough to score the preferred counsel table next to the windows that looked out over Fagatogo and the harbor. From the window I could see Hertrudes in one of her usual haunts under a huge tree. She looked intent digging in the dirt. She had danced through my dreams the night before: she'd been skipping down the beach at Alega, holding an open briefcase over her head. Paper money, looking sparkly in the moonlit night, streamed out of the briefcase and blew all over the silvery sand.

The spectator section of the courtroom was bursting. Everyone was there—our clients, Adeline and Catherine, friends, members of the Concerned Citizen's Coalition, and the media. We saw a few midlevel employees of the American Samoa government posted here and there and sensed their animosity. Several of the Samoan factory workers were also in the courtroom and sat with their huge arms crossed. When

Christa and I turned around and peeked at them, they were scowling.

The gist of our case was this: we were trying to prove that Kil-Soo Lee and Daewoosa Samoa, Ltd., along with Tour Company 12 and International Manpower Supply (apparently operated and controlled wholly by the Vietnamese government) owed our clients the wages promised in their contracts. This involved establishing that they both were "jointly and severally" responsible for those payments, and that those payments had not been made as promised: a basic breach-of-contract action. We also wanted to prove that Lee (et al.) were responsible for assaulting our clients, depriving them of food and adequate housing, taking and holding their passports, restricting their freedom, and various other nasty and potentially criminal acts.

The plaintiffs (about twenty Chinese gentlemen) were represented by attorney Afoa Su'esu'e Lutu. He didn't attend the trial but for one afternoon. With his and the court's permission, Christa and I essentially rolled their case into ours, since the facts were largely identical.

Lee, through his lawyers Marie Lafaele and Aitofele T. Sunia (the governor's brother) defended against our allegations by taking the stance that it was really *another* Daewoosa: USA Daewoosa (occasionally referenced as Daewoosa Korea) that had done these things, not *this* Daewoosa. Ah yes, the old "it was really my identical twin" defense. They maintained that USA Daewoosa and Daewoosa Samoa were different entities, and that was that. They argued that none of the alleged acts were to be blamed on them, and if the acts even happened, it was the workers' fault. We considered these arguments nonsense. It remained to be seen whether the court did as well.

Tourism Company 12 was represented by Paul Miller. He would try to establish that whatever happened at the factory was solely Lee's fault, and they had no responsibility or control and thus were not liable. IMS was not represented.

Christa and I had accumulated so much paper and exhibits around this case it was staggering. We kept some of the more notable documents and reminders with us on our counsel table. Prior to the trial Christa had mentioned to one of our most supportive friends, the incredible artist Catherine Buchanan, that she wasn't feeling overly tough. Catherine crafted Christa a teeny weeny violin case to remind her that she was as tough as a gangster. (For those too young to remember, there was a series of Hollywood movies that depicted Chicago gangsters carrying their tommy guns in violin cases.) We kept it on the counsel table every day throughout the trial. It inspired us.

The bailiff called us to stand and Justice Richmond and Chief Associate Judge Logoa'i filed in and took their seats on the bench. As I stood for my opening statement, I rifled the wheel of the chair over my long muumuu and was yanked abruptly back down into my chair, startling myself and the judges (and perhaps setting the bizarre tone the trial would take).

What would become the longest trial in the history of American Samoa had finally begun.

In the course of the trial, we needed as many as five translators: Vietnamese, Korean, Chinese, English, and Samoan, to make sure every witness and party understood what was said. The actual in-court translation resulted in a jumbled and confused nightmare of language. Lawyers who litigated in American Samoa were already used to articulating our oral examinations and arguments into spaced, paused sentences suitable for translation breaks—but this took pausing to a new level. I have trouble pausing on a good day, and this molasses-like pace was driving me nuts (granted, a short road). Plus, because we had to scramble, our translators were less than experienced and tended to lapse back into the third person when supposed to be translating directly.

BITS AND PIECES

I was reading a book recently about Sacajawea, the young Indian woman who helped Lewis and Clark in their great Corps of Discovery of the American West 196 years ago.

At one point the book described how Lewis and Clark communicated with a group of Shoshone Indians. Sacajawea would translate from Shoshone to Hidatsa, a Frenchman who spoke Hidatsa would translate the Hidatsa to French, and then another palagi would translate from French to English.

Shoshone to Hidatsa to French to English and then back again.

Yesterday I was sitting in the upstairs courtroom at the High Court of American Samoa. Around me I could hear various people speaking in Samoan, English, Korean, Vietnamese, and Chinese.

At one point Kil-Soo Lee, owner of Daewoosa, was called to testify. But the Korean translator had left the courthouse, so Mr. Lee could not testify. While the attorneys were pulling their hair out at this delay, a Chinese man entered the room. This fellow apparently speaks Korean in addition to Chinese, so there was some thought about corralling him into working as a translator for Mr. Lee.

The only problem: the man didn't speak English (very well). It was suggested that was not an insurmountable problem because Christa Lin (an attorney representing some Vietnamese workers) speaks the same Chinese dialect as the Chinese man.

If this arrangement had been used, questions to Mr. Lee from attorneys would have gone from English to Chinese to Korean and then back to English. The questions themselves would have been made on behalf of Vietnamese clients, and translators would have been 1) an attorney suing Mr. Lee on behalf of Vietnamese workers, and 2) a Chinese man who was suing Mr. Lee himself (the Chinese man was represented by a different attorney, Afoa Lutu).

Sacajawea's job was no less difficult, perhaps, but I think she probably had fewer conflicts of interest.

(Mr. Lee ended up with two translators, one of which is trilingual, in Samoan, English, and Korean. So far as I'm aware, she doesn't speak any Chinese dialects, nor Hebrew or Urdu.)

—Lewis Wolman, editor, *Samoa News*, February 23, 2001

Proving that Daewoosa failed to provide our workers with nutritious meals was an important part of our case. We presented testimonial evidence through Dr. Heather Margaret that what food the workers were given was grossly below governmental (not to mention community) standards.

Prior to that, though, we had to establish what food the workers were in fact receiving, and when. To show this, we subpoenaed a Ms. Lin (not to be confused with our own heroine Christa Lin), who worked for Kil-Soo Lee in management. She worked in his office and was not a sewer on the floor; she lived separately from the other workers. My examination was only intended to establish what the workers ate and how often. I started with the "what" they were given to eat, which sounded easy enough. Who knew what cuisine-related cultural differences would loom so large and make the simplest of definitions almost impossible? As is apparent, cross-examination was beyond vexing, just figuring out what a salad was.

Cross-Examination of Ms. Lin, Daewoosa management:

MS. SUDBURY: How many days a week do the workers get salad?

MS. LIN: I think the problem is none of us know the word for "salad."

MS. SUDBURY: Well, she said salad earlier.

MS. LIN: She said something smells bad.

MS. SUDBURY: What smells bad?

MS. LIN: I'm talking about salad, the smell. She said smell.

MS. LAFAELE: She's describing.

MS. LIN: Yes, describing salad.

MR. MILLER: Sour crout?

MS. SUDBURY: Do you know what, maybe we need another translator.

MS. LAFAELE: Oh, no. I think they have translated them to now.

MS. SUDBURY: Okay. How often do the workers get salad?

MS. LAFAELE: Your Honor, if counsel could just describe what salad is?

MS. SUDBURY: She testified that they got salad. She must know what a salad is.

MS. LAFAELE: Because I heard differently.

THE COURT: Is there such a word for lettuce?

MS. SUDBURY: Let me ask a different question. You testified that the workers got salad, what did you mean by "salad"?

MS. LAFAELE: Your Honor, if this may help? When that word "salad" came out, I heard it from the translator. He said potato and then potato salad, so perhaps the translator at that time was describing chop, what is chopped potatoes, and that's how it came out that way.

THE COURT: And later you also translated as just salad?

MS. SUDBURY: It came out just salad and this came from her?

MS. LIN (to the Korean interpreter): Could you ask her that question?

MS. SUDBURY: All right. You testified that the workers got salad, what's in the salad? Let me ask this, do you know what the word "salad" means?

MS. LIN: It's Shintye Chinese. The word that they're asking her is called Shintye and that can just mean any kind of vegetables; doesn't really mean salad particularly. It just means vegetables.

MS. SUDBURY: Have you ever been to a restaurant and had a green salad?

THE COURT: That's not going to get us anywhere.

MS. SUDBURY: Do you ever serve the workers lettuce?

THE COURT: Let's just ask the question and then get an answer yes or no.

THE WITNESS: Yes.

MS. LIN: Maybe we should show pictures.

MS. SUDBURY: I don't have any pictures of lettuce.

Not my finest hour, but a girl does the best she can with what she has to work with.

Madam Mai (*hhwwiiick*—Christa and I restrained ourselves from making the slicing motion across our throats when in open court) testified extensively at trial. We began our examination by asking her about the April 25, 2000, "direct order" from the Vietnam National Administration of Tourism.

Excerpts of testimony of Madam Mai, January 19, 2001:

MS. SUDBURY: Ms. Mai, I'd like to show you what's been marked as Exhibit No. 21. Can you look at that exhibit, please, and tell the court what it is?

MADAM MAI: This document was signed by the director of Tour Company 12.

MS. SUDBURY: And this document was sent to Mr. Minh and all workers of Daewoosa from Hanoi; is that correct? Yes or no?

MADAM MAI: This is for Mr. Minh, who is the manager of the workers here.

MS. SUDBURY: And doesn't this letter order the workers to stop with the lawsuit, to stop everything and not appear in court? Is that correct?

MADAM MAI: To my understanding, this letter put us in the situation of mediation between the problems that the workers might have with Company Daewoosa.

MS. SUDBURY: Ms. Mai, yes or no. Does this—

MR. MILLER: Your Honor, I think the conduct of counsel needs to be objected to as harassment as counsel—ask counsel to please sit down and quit intimidating the witness.

THE COURT: I don't think she's doing that.

MS. SUDBURY: Ms. Mai, does this letter tell the workers not to participate in the lawsuit? Yes or no?

MADAM MAI: She say that she—I am not so sure what is the English translation provided to you stated, but I'm reading the Vietnamese.

MS. SUDBURY: I would draw your attention to partway through paragraph number one, about halfway through.

MADAM MAI: I look at this as an advice.

I rolled my eyes at Christa. Advice? *Really?*

Further Excerpts of testimony of Madam Mai, January 19, 2001:

MS. SUDBURY: Did each worker give Tour Company 12 six thousand dollars to come here and work?

MADAM MAI: Never.

MS. SUDBURY: Never. How much did each worker give you, total?

MADAM MAI: Is nearly three thousand.

MS. SUDBURY: Nearly three thousand?

MADAM MAI: Yes.

MS. SUDBURY: And that's all the money they gave you, total money; right?

MADAM MAI: Not excluding the deposit. Nearly three thousand excluding deposit. Excluding the deposit and the ticket they have to buy.

MS. SUDBURY: So three thousand plus the deposit— Ms. Mai, plus the airfare—is that right?—three thousand—

MADAM MAI: I'm sorry. Three thousand including the airfares but excluding the deposit.

MS. SUDBURY: And the deposit was one thousand dollars; correct?

MADAM MAI: Yes.

MS. SUDBURY: And did that also include the two hundred sixty-four dollars business fee?

MADAM MAI: Yes.

MS. SUDBURY: And the five hundred dollars service fee?

At that point Madam Mai started giving the translator a ration of grief in agitated Vietnamese, and no one understood what was going on so we recessed. It was lunchtime, anyway.

Another interesting witness was Um Hee, the ostensible president of Daewoosa Korea and also widely rumored to be the mistress of Kil-Soo Lee. Ms. Hee came to Pago Pago from Korea a few months prior to trial and apparently lent great support and succor to Kil-Soo Lee. She was always present at court and was often seen whispering with Lee and his counsel.

Excerpts from testimony of Ms. Um Hee:
MS. SUDBURY: Good morning, Ms. Hee. Do you go by Ms. Hee?

MS. UM HEE: Um.

MS. SUDBURY: Ms. Um?

MS. UM: Yes.

MS. SUDBURY: Okay. Does it make you nervous if I stand up when I talk to you?

MS. UM: No. It's okay.

MS. SUDBURY: All right. Just checking. Thank you. Now, just so I'm clear, so I understand your testimony. Are you saying that you're the president of USA Daewoosa, and USA Daewoosa has no relationship

with Daewoosa Samoa; is that your testimony?
MS. LAFAELE: Your Honor, objection.
MS. SUDBURY: Based on what?
MS. LAFAELE: Objection. She has stated that they have had a connection. They've sold materials.
THE COURT: Let her ask the question and get an answer. It's cross-examination.
MS. SUDBURY: Do you want me to ask it again?
MS. UM: That's okay.
MS. SUDBURY: You want me to ask it again?
THE INTERPRETER: Yes.
MS. SUDBURY: Is it your testimony that you're the president of USA Daewoosa, and Daewoosa Samoa has no connection with USA Daewoosa?
MS. UM: Yeah. Just we have some or few of the business connection only, not the direct connection.
MS. SUDBURY: But Daewoosa—USA Daewoosa—didn't sign any of these labor contracts or work to get laborers here for Daewoosa Samoa; is that correct?
MS. UM: Yes. That's correct

And so on.

Excerpts of testimony from Ms. Huang:
MS. SUDBURY: And you were involved in payroll?
MS. HUANG: Yes.
MS. SUDBURY: And were the plaintiff workers paid on the eighth or twelfth of every month?
MS. HUANG: There were sometimes—
MS. SUDBURY: Yes or no?
MS. HUANG: Sometimes the money came in early and sometimes the money came in late.

MS. SUDBURY: Were there ever months the workers were not paid? Yes or no.
MS. HUANG: They've been paid.
MS. SUDBURY: Every month?
MS. HUANG: But delayed. Every month.
MS. SUDBURY: They received money every month?
MS. HUANG: Not quite on time if that was what you were referring to.
MS. SUDBURY: Have there been months when the plaintiff workers were not paid? Yes or no.
MS. HUANG: Yes, there were some.

Our cross-examination of Kil-Soo Lee was beyond excruciating. He didn't wear his fancy suit and instead wore a casual shirt and trousers, no tie. We figured he was going for the riches-to-rags pathetic poor person effect. He had lately given up trying to shake my hand but still bowed to Christa. I generally narrowed my eyes when I looked at him; Rob said I looked like a third grader pissed at her friend on the playground, and not the least bit scary.

The galling part was that even through the trial, Lee never lost his smugness. His parents apparently never said to him, "And you wipe that look off your face right now, mister, or they'll be hell to pay." By the time of trial, we had hauled his sorry ass into court more than fourteen times in the past year and had prevailed each time. But he knew that this would be just one more hearing, one more occasion for him to stave off punishment.

We had put the Daewoosa garment factory into receivership. Lee was no longer able to send the workers home but didn't care. He was impervious, or so he thought. We hadn't been able to locate any money of Lee's and surmised that his money had been safely sent back to Korea. At one point our intrepid workers found an abandoned shipping canister with an open and empty safe inside. Speculation was rampant about what Lee had done with the thousands and thousands of dollars that he had realized from the operation of the factory (if they existed).

I, on the other hand, was slowly learning what would eventually be the lesson I will never forget: don't take it personally. These are not my facts. Now I am able to not wake up at three in the morning and fuss over the dire straits of a client. Now if the phone rings in the middle of the night and it's not a member of my family, I don't answer it. Now I tell my clients I will fight for them and perform my best advocacy on their behalf, but my heart is my own. Most importantly, though, there is no way I ever want to hate a person that much again; it is just too painful.

But then I didn't know that. At the Daewoosa trial with Lee on the stand, it was nothing *but* personal for me. This man was responsible for traumatizing almost three hundred people, for lying to them and taking them away from their families and countries under false pretenses, for stealing from them, for abusing them, for keeping them under his evil, dictatorial thumb until they had lost faith in tomorrow. If not for him Dung and Nga would likely be still alive, Quyen would see out of both her eyes, Hang would have all his hearing, and the world would be a better place. But such is not how lessons are given.

Christa and I had discussed who would conduct Lee's cross-examination. We decided I would—if I kept my temper down. I managed to get through the examination without throwing my pen at his smirk-ridden face, although there were some close calls. He would answer my easier questions in fluent English without the need of a translator and then suddenly became unable to articulate the words "yes" or "no" in English. I drew numbers on the easel indicating the amounts that he had taken from our clients. He grinned and shrugged his shoulders.

As the examination went on, Lee relied more on his translator, which was another exercise in frustration. Translators were there to relay verbatim what the witness said, not to speak in the third person. However, since we were unable to hire an actual professional, we did the best we could with what we had.

Excerpts of testimony from Kil-Soo Lee:

MS. SUDBURY: Let's talk a little bit about Daewoosa, all right?

MR. LEE: Yes.

MS. SUDBURY: Are there any other owners of Daewoosa?

MR. LEE: No. No other owners.

MS. SUDBURY: And are there any shareholders or stockholders in Daewoosa?

MR. LEE: He try to making shareholder, but he could not make it.

MS. SUDBURY: So you're the sole owner of Daewoosa; is that correct?

MR. LEE: Practically his own company. Yeah, practically. Actually. Actually. Because the different size company, but actually his own company. Private company. Because nobody invest.

MS. SUDBURY: That's fine, Mr. Lee.

MR. LEE: Whenever he need the money from Korea, all they can use only his name as a receiver. Give the money to his company only his name.

And so on, ad nauseum. Extraction of testimony from Kil-Soo Lee was minutely tortuous. He did admit that he withheld FICA (Social Security) from the workers' paychecks yet failed to pay the US government those withheld amounts. He admitted that he failed to pay the America Samoa Power Authority and that ASPA shut off the electricity at the factory compound because of the outstanding arrearage. He testified to these facts and didn't seem to register the impropriety of his acts. He was Teflon.

The biggest nexus we had to prove was that Daewoosa Samoa was the same entity as USA Daewoosa. Lee maintained steadfastly that they were different corporations—despite the fact that they had the same members of the board, officers, employees, and shared bank accounts. It was just the most inane argument we had heard.

Along about this time, midway through trial, Paul Miller—who represented Tour Company 12—decided to try to represent several of the workers. Since they were already represented by Christa and me, his shenanigans presented both ethical and procedural barriers to doing so. When we found out that he had contacted our clients—a huge ethical no-no—we jumped up and down (legally speaking, in Christa's case; literally speaking, in mine) and brought this to the attention of the court. Prior to the separate motion hearing on Paul's nonsensical move, Christa and I met Paul in the courthouse law library and tried to convince him that his actions were both highly unethical and supremely idiotic. He disagreed and we three had a big ol' screaming come-apart right there in the library. This is where I learned I did not always have to take the lead in arguments, and also where I learned that if you pissed off the usually mild-mannered Christa Lin, she would get in your face and roar like a dragon.

Lee called Nu'uuli Ioane to the stand. He was the floor manager who'd had words with Quyen the day of the riot, dutifully reported the threats of Kil-Soo Lee to the Samoan workers, and had encouraged them to beat the Vietnamese. As he was a *fa'afafine*, I was unsure of the political niceties in crossing him. I took my cue from Marie Lee's counsel.

Excerpts from testimony of Elekana Nu'uuli Ioane:
MS. LAFAELE: Would you please state your name for the record?
MR. IOANE: My name is Elekana Nu'uuli Ioane.
MS. LAFAELE: Mr. Ioane, where do you live?
MR. IOANE: On the village of Nu'uuli.
MS. LAFAELE: And are you an employee of Daewoosa or in the management of Daewoosa?
MR. IOANE: Well, I was assistant production manager at Daewoosa.
MS. LAFAELE: Okay. Do you oversee security also at Daewoosa?
MR. IOANE: Yes.

Cross-examination by Ms. Sudbury:
MS. SUDBURY: Now, was there ever a curfew imposed on the workers by Daewoosa?

MR. IOANE: No.

MS. SUDBURY: As you know we're hearing testimony of Vietnamese that there was a curfew imposed by Daewoosa of ten o'clock. What is this—do you have any idea what they're referring to?

MR. IOANE: Well, actually the curfew, it was based on the village curfew of Nu'uuli. We have—we've been explain it to Mr. Lee and Malaetasi was explain that to him too. The village of Nu'uuli have a curfew, and it's about nine thirty at night the *aumaaga* will ride their trucks and blow the shells. We call it *foafoa* around the village. So that's a warning for everybody to be no more roaming on the street after ten o'clock. But the curfew is at ten o'clock. And then Mr. Lee was explaining to the translator, Vietnamese and Chinese, to explain it to the workers; they have to respect the curfew. But there was no enforcement in curfew for at Daewoosa.

MS. SUDBURY: Okay. Is it posted anywhere—I mean how do people live in Nu'uuli know about this curfew?

MR. IOANE: Well, I remember the council, the *matai* committee, had a meeting, and then they posted all over in stores in the village in Nu'uuli. All stores have rules of this curfew.

I remember immediately after we opened, our grand opening, and this is probably around May of '99. And Malaetasi was explain it to Mr. Lee and that time there was a lot of complaining from the village people about the Vietnamese roaming around and trespassing their property very late at night, picking up fruits. And so they complaining about, and this is after late. It's after midnight. So Malaetasi was explain it to Mr. Lee the village is enforcing a curfew. So ten o'clock everybody should be inside.

MS. SUDBURY: Okay. What happens if a worker arrives after ten o'clock? What would the security do?

MR. IOANE: Well, there's a lot of Vietnamese coming in after ten o'clock. What we do, we just let them in. Sometimes some of these men, they come in drunk and belligerent and try—they try to take bottles of beer in their dorm. We stop them, and we told them if they want to finish their beer, they can sit not outside the gate but inside the compound and finish their beer before they go to their rooms.

MS. SUDBURY: Why would you have them finish their beer inside the gate rather than outside?

MR. IOANE: Well, for their safety. It's because the *aumaaga* is sort of patrolling around the street at that time. So if they find anybody drinking or sitting, you know, on the street, and then will be—I don't know what they will do.

MS. SUDBURY: Okay. And what was the purpose for Mr. Lee agreeing to tell the workers to respect the village curfew?

MR. IOANE: Well, Mr. Lee was trying to protect—it's for their safety because he was saying they don't want to be beat up or get raped after very late hours of the night.

MS. SUDBURY: Outside the—

MR. IOANE: Outside the compound.

MS. SUDBURY: Is that village curfew—is that for adults as well as children?

MR. IOANE: It's for everyone.

MS. SUDBURY: So no one is allowed in the village of Nu'uuli on the streets after ten o'clock?

MR. IOANE: Not allowed to roaming on the street, drunk on the street, or make noise.

MS. SUDBURY: So no one is allowed to walk on the streets of Nu'uuli after ten o'clock; is that—

MR. IOANE: After ten o'clock, yes.

MS. SUDBURY: That's the law?

MR. IOANE: That's the curfew of the village, not the law.

MS. SUDBURY: And that extends to seven o'clock the next morning?

MR. IOANE: No. Close to eleven and twelve o'clock at night. It's for—to protect a lot of stores being broken in and all those things. So that is the curfew—the village enforcing that curfew to prevent those things happening. Like twelve to one o'clock?

MS. SUDBURY: So it's okay to roam around three in the morning?

MR. IOANE: That's very late. Somebody might get raped or beat up.

Nga v. Daewoosa, originally scheduled for two days, continued for five long and anxiety-filled weeks. Fortunately, we were not continuously in court the entire five weeks; we got sandwiched in between the regular docket. Christa and I had all but moved into Justice Richmond's courtroom. We left Christa's wee violin case and other accoutrements in the courtroom. The entire High Court courtroom docket had to be tediously rearranged, and the clerks were not pleased. District court was held in the law library instead of its courtroom and District Court Judge John Ward was not pleased. Rumor had it the chief justice himself was not pleased. The trial went so, so slowly. Justice Richmond, always the picture of calm, looked frayed; Judge Logoa'i just swiveled his high-backed chair around and faced the harbor. We suspected he was sleeping.

Our lives *were* this lawsuit; we were on a small boat in the middle of a great ocean in bad weather and couldn't get off even if we had wanted to. We spent our days in the courtroom and our evenings dissecting the day's trial events and writing endless drafts of our closing argument.

Three weeks into the trial, the *New York Times* published a bombshell of an article that incited great passion in the territory, mostly negative, and mostly against us. The article, "Beatings and Other Abuses Cited at Samoan Apparel Plant That Supplied US Retailers," told of a US Labor Department investigation that uncovered an "extraordinary variety of abuses" at the Daewoosa factory. We felt partially vindicated and were thus unprepared for the open hostility we received. We were accused of planting the article, of lying, but the worse accusation was that we were being anti-Samoan. Our most serious offense was the culturally *unpardonable* sin of giving American Samoa a "black eye" internationally. I did not understand this emotion as I had been raised to question authority and point out perceived wrongs. The American Samoan governor angrily disputed the article and called it "bull." We got more threats and late-night telephone hang ups.

We plodded along through witnesses and testimony and posturing throughout the remainder of the trial. We were fast running out of outfits to wear to court. Many other items had joined Catherine's tiny violin case on our counsel table, including notes of encouragement and inspiration from friends and clients. Our boxes of files lived in Justice Richmond's upstairs courtroom for those five weeks, pushed into a corner when other hearings took place and dragged out for us. We finished up with our witnesses and got the evidence before the court that could, we hoped, prove our case. At the beginning of the trial we had planned on introducing a slim binder of exhibits. By the time trial ended we had three full boxes. On the last day of testimony Justice Richmond requested that we submit our closing arguments in writing instead of presenting them orally. I sometimes think he just could not bear for this to continue any longer. At last the grueling trial was over. We filed our closing arguments and waited for the decision. We would wait fourteen months.

The day after trial we relaxed with the workers in the deserted cafeteria at the Daewoosa factory compound. The room was large and sunny and appended onto the kitchen. There were rows of long tables, like a typical cafeteria. The walls were painted yellow. At one end of the room there were huge black letters written on the wall, in Vietnamese. I asked the workers what the letters meant; it seemed a strange place for such an imperious-looking message. They giggled behind their hands before they told me; perhaps they knew I would laugh outrageously—and way too loudly—when they finally did. It translated to "Be Quiet."

Chapter Eleven—I Am the Mouth, Screaming

The *Samoa News* still carried frequent articles about the Vietnamese workers. Safe in Honolulu, the Southern Baptist Convention, through Stanley Togikawa, helped Quyen obtain a glass eye. A large group of locals continued to help the workers with food and work when they could. Twenty-six of the workers were baptized at Lions Park, Tafuna. In February 2001, the paper reported the scandalous news that the workers' babies were US nationals, just like American Samoans. However, the ASG attorney general pointed out that the existence of an infant US national need not interfere with deportation proceedings for the child's mother.

A few months before the trial, in October 2000, the United States Congress passed something called the Trafficking Victim's Protection Act. Since Christa and I were not astutely tuned into the daily workings of our federal Congress, we had no idea such a thing existed.

However, other people did. Before the trial, a far-sighted, brilliant, and especially kind man named Grover Joseph Rees, and his equally astute wife, Lan Dai Nguyen, visited the island. I had known Lan Dai because she had telephonically interviewed me regularly for her Asia Pacific Radio Show over the past year. Joseph was the former chief justice of the High Court of American Samoa. He'd been replaced by Michael Kruse several years prior.

Apparently, this Trafficking Victim's Protection Act was something that could possibly help our Vietnamese clients. They were stuck between Vietnam and the United States and apparently not welcomed by either. Joseph and Lan Dai told us that the Trafficking Victim's Protection Act had been passed to help estranged foreign workers in their position. It was an incredibly long shot, since the act had just passed a few months before and was not tested yet. We had no idea how it worked or how to help our clients apply, though; it was singularly unknown to us.

FORMER CHIEF JUSTICE SPEAKS OUT ON DAEWOOSA WORKERS

Some Daewoosa Samoa workers have existed in a form of "slavery," according to former American Samoa Chief Justice Grover Joseph Rees.

Now a legal counsel for the US House Subcommittee on Human Rights, Judge Rees was recently quoted in the *Orange County* [southern California newspaper] *Register* regarding the Daewoosa debacle.

Rees, who was on-island two weeks ago investigating the Daewoosa situation told the *Register* the workers might be eligible for something like asylum under a new US law that grants harbor to victims of human trafficking.

Daewoosa Samoa's Vietnamese workers might qualify for a US nonimmigrant visa to reside in the United States if they can prove they are victims of a severe form of trafficking in person perpetrated by a foreign government, according to Rees.

He was referring to a new "T"-type visa, which is reserved for "Victims of Severe Forms of Trafficking in Persons."

The new T-visa allows the victim to bring her spouse and minor children (and, in the case of a worker younger than twenty-one, her parents) into the United States as well.

"There is no way to know in advance whether any particular person qualifies for this relief," Rees explained. "The person would have to prove that he or she is a victim of a severe form of trafficking in person—that is, brought by force, fraud, or coercion into slavery, involuntary servitude, or debt bondage— and would face serious harm, such as retaliation by the traffickers, if forced back to his or her home country."

—*Samoa News,* February 2, 2001

NY TIMES PLAYS UP DAEWOOSA "BEATINGS, ABUSES"

"Workers at a factory in American Samoa that made apparel for the J. C. Penney Company and other retailers were often beaten and were provided food so inadequate that some were 'walking skeletons,' a Labor Department investigation has found."

The [article] was titled "Beatings and Other Abuses Cited at Samoan Apparel Plant That Supplied US Retailers."

Regarding food, the report allegedly states, "The diet consisting primarily of a watery broth of rice and cabbage is of a type and quantity that may lead to malnutrition. Management admits they withhold meals from employees as a form of punishment when workers complain about food."

—*Samoa News,* February 7, 2001

TAUESE DISPUTES NY TIMES

"Bull!" is how Governor Tauese Sunia characterized the strongest allegations in the *New York Times* story.

Reached by the *Samoa News* yesterday afternoon, Tauese said he had not read the *New York Times* story in detail, but as he skimmed over it, he disputed point after point.

The governor recalled three surprise and one scheduled visits he had made to Daewoosa and said the workers were being fed properly. "I ate the lunch myself, and they did not know ahead of time I was coming."

He said he was not aware of any beatings, except for the November 28, 2000, skirmish, and said the workers each had their own beds.

—*Samoa News,* February 7, 2001

BITS AND PIECES: AMERICAN SAMOA IS LIKE A RAG DOLL
For the average reader, I assume the never-ending series

of stories about Daewoosa Samoa can be quite boring. But I am finding them increasingly interesting, and so should anyone interested in American Samoa's economic and political status.

It seems clear that American Samoa is just a "rag doll" to the major players in the saga. The major players came from Korea, Vietnam, and China. The minor players were from American Samoa. We were just a rag doll.

At yesterday's closing day of the month-long trial, Daewoosa owner Kil-Soo Lee testified that a board of directors meeting held in 1998 included three men with Korean names and Mary Tulafono, and Mrs. Tulafono wasn't formally removed from the board until June 1, 2000. He said that action was memorialized in a set of minutes written by his attorney at the time, Aitofele Sunia.

His attorney now is Marie Lafaele, who took over from Sunia, who took over from Malaetasi Togafau, who took over from Togiola Tulafono (who was a senator at the time).

He also said [Kil-Soo Lee] was now the sole owner of Daewoosa and some of the company stock he owned had been purchased by him from Togiola Tulafono and (separately) Mary Tulafono in 1998 (before the garment plant went into operations).

He said he had not originally been part of the company (which, incidentally, was originally formed to be a cardboard box manufacturer) but had come in later, in 1998, and that Togiola Tulafono (who was lieutenant governor in 1998) had been one of his immigration sponsors.

Not that I want to contradict Mr. Lee, but I doubt Mrs. Tulafono was a member of the board until June 1, 2000, and I doubt she attended a board meeting in

October 1998 (two years after her husband became lieutenant governor).

I have no idea if he did in fact pay money to the "Tulafonos" for shares in the company, whether he owns the entire company himself at this point, or whether it is true, as he states, that he put $5 million of his own money into the bankrupt company.

But that's the point; the whole saga is filled with out-and-out contradictions that no one can easily reconcile. It's not merely that some people are lying (although that seems an inescapable conclusion) as that the whole matter is so confusing (perhaps purposefully) that "getting to the bottom of things" is virtually impossible.

The thing that seems clear to me is that American Samoa was a pawn, or more accurately, a rag doll. We were used and abused because we have our own immigration laws, our own taxation laws, and our own corporation and business laws and yet we can host a "Made in the USA" label and provide a platform for duty- and quota-free access to the US market for goods by people from the communist republics of China and Vietnam.

And we host an American-style court system replete with "due process" protections and can host applications for T-visa political asylum requests, and babies born here are entitled to US passports.

I don't like feeling like a rag doll, and I think Daewoosa should serve as a cautionary tale about the ways in which our unique status can be manipulated by people with motives that don't necessarily take into account the welfare of the territory.

—Lewis Wolman, editor, *Samoa News,*
February 23, 2001

We tried a last-ditch effort to get the workers home. We appealed to Paul Miller to prevail on his client, TC12, to cough up the money and send the workers back to Vietnam. It seemed the least they could do.

MONEY TO SEND VIETNAMESE WORKERS HOME NO LONGER AVAILABLE

Yesterday, *Samoa News* spoke to attorney Paul Miller, who represents Tour Company Number 12 (TourCo 12). TourCo 12 is a recruitment agency in Vietnam that works closely (or perhaps under) the Vietnamese government.

Miller says TourCo 12 turned over to Daewoosa a total of $450,000 for the 250 workers they recruited ($1,800 each). Well, it's time to go, but Daewoosa doesn't have the money, and neither does ASG.

—Samoa News, February 23, 2001

In early March of 2001 the miracles began. The FBI's quiet investigation into the Daewoosa mess had paid off in a completely unforeseen and astounding way. The miracles first appeared in the form of two avenging angels, Susan Lynn French and Robert Moossy. In their day jobs they were actually seasoned and highly respected prosecutors with the United States Department of Justice, but they remain angels to me. They arrived on a night flight to Pago Pago along with more FBI agents and went to work. They met with us and they met with the workers. Then they told us that the US government had granted something called "significant public benefit parole" to more than two hundred of our Vietnamese workers. This meant that the workers would be legally allowed into the United States. Just like that; just that quickly.

Now here was a stunning and fortuitous turn of events. The workers would be flown to Hawaii and thereafter to receptive places throughout the United States. The workers were then eligible for the newly enacted T-visa for victims of slave trafficking and involuntary servitude. They would now be safe and off the island. It was a big giant miracle.

The first group of workers left the island for the United States in late-March 2001. We knew they were headed for a much better life and would have the "chances" they sought all along. There were about twenty or so workers on the airline flight to Honolulu.

Christa was also on that flight. She'd had enough of American Samoa and was ready for another adventure. She planned on going to Chicago, where she had scored a great job with the Equal Employment Opportunity Commission. (I was envious, since I had gone to law school in Chicago and knew how fabulous that city is.) She had sailed through this Daewoosa experience with grace, and she had softened my abruptness and anger. She had lent her considerable intellectual skills to this lawsuit for free, and those skills largely carried the day. When she got on the plane to Honolulu in March, she looked not a day older than when she had arrived more than two years before, but she looked so very much wiser.

It surely was hard to see her go. When Rob and I went to the airport to say good-bye to Christa and the workers, little pieces of our hearts flew away into the night.

VIETNAMESE WORKERS FLYING TO UNITED STATES, NOT VIETNAM

Saturday night's Hawaiian Air flight reportedly carried twenty Vietnamese workers, plus one of the four infants born to a Vietnamese worker while she was living here.

Samoa News was unable to learn on what legal or financial basis the foreigners are being admitted to the United States, but it appears the US Department of Justice is paving the way for the workers to settle, at least temporarily, in the United States so they will be available to testify as witnesses should the ongoing criminal investigation into Daewoosa result in federal prosecutions.

Such prosecutions would have to be conducted in the United States because there is no federal court of jurisdiction here.

Meanwhile, there are still two FBI agents and an attorney from the US Department of Justice on-island conducting their investigation.

—*Samoa News,* March 20, 2001

TAUESE DISTURBED BY LACK OF RESPECT

"I am disappointed by the lack of courtesy and respect being shown to the governor of this territory by officials of the federal government," Governor Tauese Sunia told *Samoa News* yesterday.

The governor said that as of yesterday afternoon, he still has not been briefed about the activities of the FBI, Department of Justice, and Immigration and Naturalization Service in relocating former Daewoosa workers to the United States.

The governor is worried that the activities of the federal government might damage the agreement he made with Vietnam's ambassador to the United States. That agreement called for Vietnam to pay for the transportation of all the workers back to Vietnam.

But now that the US government (which was not a party to that agreement) has stepped in and facilitated the movement of the Vietnam nationals to the United States (without the involvement of their communist government), Tauese fears his agreement may be undermined.

—*Samoa News,* March 22, 2001

Flailing politically, Tauese Sunia stated publicly that "you know and I know nothing happened at Daewoosa." On April 17, 2001, he was quoted in the *Samoa News*: "We've got to close the door and be more mindful and be more selective of who we allow into this territory and under what terms. Consequently, your government has decided to put the garment industry on record that it will be a while, and it's going to take a lot of convincing, before we look in to this area of business again, importation of foreign workers."

Still, we wondered why those two FBI agents were still on-island.

Chapter Twelve—
Unfettered and Alive

KIL-SOO LEE ARRESTED IN Nu'uuli; BEING HELD IN HONOLULU

Two FBI agents arrested Kil-Soo Lee, the Korean owner and president of Daewoosa Samoa Friday afternoon, on American Samoa soil. He is presently in federal custody and will appear tomorrow before a federal court to answer criminal charges today or tomorrow.

The local government has never investigated Mr. Lee for criminal charges, and the civil lawsuit against Lee was brought by the workers. The American Samoa government has never tried to corral Mr. Lee through legal means.

—Samoa News, March 26, 2001

In addition to the obvious, here is why Kil-Soo Lee's arrest was so unbelievably cool. Never, in the history of American Samoa, has the US government arrested a person on territorial soil. In a stunning precedent, the FBI arrested Kil-Soo Lee and hauled him back to the nearest federal court (which was in Honolulu) to stand trial for a number of criminal acts, including involuntary servitude, bribery, money laundering, and trafficking in humans. The workers would be material witnesses at that trial.

I cannot overstate how delicious this moment was. The photo that the *Samoa News* ran of Lee after his unexpected arrest was taken as he was being escorted to the plane. It was delightful. His mouth was open in an O and he had the look on his face I'd wanted to see for months. It said, "The jig, she is up."

However, the American Samoa government was not as pleased as we were. They filed a bizarre objection with the Supreme Court of the United States and protested the arrest, alleging the federal government lacked proper jurisdiction to arrest Lee on territorial soil and challenging taking him to the federal court in Honolulu. I found this tactic inexplicable, as Tutuila was in fact a territory of the *United States.* Reassuringly, the Supremes failed to grant certiorari, and the arrest stood.

SEVERAL THINGS TO MAKE ME QUEASY
COMMENTARY BY *SAMOA NEWS* EDITOR
LEWIS WOLMAN

Governor Tauese is mad at the federal government, but he ought to be grateful that the US attorney general didn't raise questions before the national press corps as to how Kil-Soo Lee got away with subjecting a few hundred women to inhumane living and working conditions, in a context that added up to involuntary servitude, over a two year period, in American Samoa.

If we are lucky, *60 Minutes* won't show up on our

doorstep and push a microphone in front of a bunch of our government officials and ask why, why, why.

The workers reportedly believed that Mr. Lee had some sort of official protection, of the sort they are familiar with, coming from a communist regime like Vietnam. They say that it appeared to them that Lee could control the police, the immigration, the courts, and the other agents of power. They saw if they complained, Lee called in the police to arrest them and had the immigration officials deport them as "troublemakers."

Lee apparently reinforced that idea through various means. Whether he had protection, or just got away with things, I don't know. But it certainly appears that he got away with things, and among the things he seems to have gotten away with was not having to post $500,000 worth of immigration bonds; deportation of the women who complained about the conditions of the factory, having the police focus their attention on the complainers instead of the company; not paying workers for months at a time; charging workers for their employment contract; not abiding by court orders; unilaterally changing the terms of the employment contract to halve the pay the workers received when he paid them anything; and squirreling away money that rightly belonged to the workers and/or ASG.

—*Samoa News,* March 29, 2001

VIRGINIA SUDBURY RESIGNS FROM U'UNA'I LEGAL SERVICES POST

Virginia Sudbury, the executive director of U'una'i Legal Services Clinic, has tendered her letter of resignation to the board of directors. She and U'una'i have engendered some controversy, but it is not known if that had any bearing on her decision to resign.

Sudbury is off-island at present and therefore not available for comment.

—*Samoa News,* March 13, 2001

Off-island, indeed: Robbie and I were some eighty miles across the water to the west, on the island of Apia, Western Samoa, at the Coconut's Beach Resort. We were drinking mai tais and trying to restore what little was left of my sanity. I had finally (really) quit smoking halfway through the Daewoosa trial: I needed something that I had control over and that alone was left to me. I was at the end of my rope and all I wanted was to be shut of this case and the island and go someplace where we could drive more than seventeen miles in one direction. I was too visible and I wanted to be anonymous. Rob still loved the island life; I would rather have eaten a bug than stay there. By that time I hated almost everything about the island. If it was not for Robbie, a few friends, and yoga, I would have not survived.

Over the next months, Rob and I repeated the airport scene thrice more with the remainder of the workers. When the last group of workers left for Honolulu, we waved enviously to the plane as it flew off.

Rob and I finally left the island of Tutuila, American Samoa, on June 21, 2001: the winter solstice in the Southern Hemisphere when we left, the summer solstice in the Northern Hemisphere when we arrived on the US mainland. Before we left the island, we had purchased property close to Rob's parents in Salt Lake City, where he had grown up. We had a place to go.

We packed up our kitties, Janey and Zuzu, to bring them back with us to Utah. Unexpectedly, this required that we obtain little kitty passports for them and cough up $150 a leg (of the flight trips, not the kitties). Since we had to fly from Pago Pago to Honolulu and Honolulu to Los Angeles and Los Angeles to Salt Lake, the costs were not inconsiderable. We had bought groovy hard-sided cat carriers back in March and left them, opened, in the living room of the little yellow house so Janey and Zuzu would get used to them. Right before we left I ripped one of my *ie lavalavas* in half and put one half in each carrier so they would have my smell.

We deposited our kitties and our luggage at the Pago Pago airport and sat in the waiting room until we boarded the plane. Several of our friends had come to see us off; I would miss some of them dearly. It was almost dark when the plane left and we flew east, so it became darker fast. I leaned my head against the window and watched lights of Tutuila as we left them behind. When the lights were below us and the window turned black, I could see my reflection in the window. I was smiling.

I have never traveled well and was beyond distressed by this trip and the ensuing separation trauma with our kitties, but Janey and Zuzu squirted out of the odd-sized baggage chute in Los Angeles looking happy to see us and none the worse for wear. When we tried to board our plane from LA to Salt Lake, we were told we had to keep the cats under our seats, but our hard carriers would not fit, so we hurriedly bought some soft carriers and stuffed our sweet and patient little kitties into them. They flew to Salt Lake, one under each of our seats. They fussed a bit and got no pretzels or beverages, but I was no longer distraught now that I had twelve hours of flying behind me and was off that island and our little family was together and going someplace safe.

We settled in cosmopolitan Salt Lake City. In the ensuing fourteen months that we waited for the High Court's decision, literally not a day passed that the lawsuit was not on my mind. Rob and I and the kitties were now safe in our home. Our clients were now ensconced in safe homes throughout the United States, but our obligation to them continued (and still does to this day). Although Kil-Soo Lee's arrest by the FBI and subsequent criminal trial by the US Department of Justice had partially vindicated us, it certainly did not put money in our clients' pockets. The High Court of American Samoa is technically unable to consider any evidence not properly presented at the trial, so the arrest and criminal charges could not affect their deliberations. We had *all* invested blood, sweat, and tears in this case, and the workers deserved a victorious outcome. Christa and I telephoned each other frequently, wondering and speculating when the decision would come out, whether our clients would prevail and be awarded damages—and if so, how much. A year after the trial ended we still had no decision. The lawsuit and its unknown outcome became a surreal, unreachable event that I occasionally thought I had also dreamed.

Chapter Thirteen—Keep Swimming

On April 16, 2002, in one of the largest judgments ever issued, the High Court of American Samoa found Kil-Soo Lee, Daewoosa Samoa, Tour Company 12, and International Manpower Supply (and arguably the government of Vietnam) liable for egregious acts and awarded our workers more than $3.5 million. We had asked for considerably less in back wages and were thrilled with the amount of the award.

I acted in the role of a very informal consultant to the Department of Justice for the criminal case against Lee, as I still represent the workers in a civil capacity. Our own avenging angels Susan Lynn French and Robert Moossy prosecuted Lee in federal court in Honolulu, and I watched the criminal proceedings with great interest from the sidelines. They were not only prosecuting Lee, they were setting the precedent that such acts of slavery, indenture, and abuse will not be tolerated on US soil. It amazes me that this was one of the first cases of its kind in recent history.

Kil-Soo Lee was incarcerated without bail in a federal penitentiary and stood trial in federal district court in Hawaii. On February 20, 2003, after a four-month trial, a federal jury found Lee guilty on thirteen charges of involuntary servitude, extortion, and money laundering. He was later sentenced to what will likely amount to the rest of his life in federal prison.

Two Samoan workers—floor manager Nu'uuli Ioane, and Sialava'a Fagaima, the woman who wielded the pipe that blinded Quyen—pled guilty in federal criminal court and admitted to beating the Vietnamese workers at Lee's behest. They also admitted that Virginia Soli'ai had convinced them to lie in their statements to the ASG police and prosecutors. They testified against Lee at the criminal trial. Sialava'a was sentenced to four years and three months in prison. Nu'uuli was sentenced to five years and ten months in prison.

Virginia Soliai and Robert Atimalala were acquitted.

Quyen is married and living in Hawaii and has a happy family. She stays in touch with Stanley, Christa, Tam, and us. She still parts her hair down the middle and is ready with a smart remark.

Taller Thuy lives in California and has her own sewing business; her son Robert is ten. She called us last Christmas Day. She brought her older son over from Vietnam under the TVPA. He is training in veterinary medicine.

Tam got married several years ago, and Christa, Rob, several of the workers, and I danced and sang at her wedding and were reminded of the joy life can possess. She and Phi have two sweet children. She still looks like she will burst into laughter at any moment.

We hear stories about the other workers, who by and large have been assimilated into life in the United States and from all accounts seem to be enjoying their days.

Christa moved to Chicago and met a nice smart man named Jonas Zamora. They fell in love and got married. They moved to Phoenix and have two beautiful babies. She is Chief Administrative Law Judge for the EEOC (Acting). She is a joy in this world.

I smile and laugh all the time now, like I used to, although I'm still too loud and tend to not blend in. Rob and I are working and growing and not looking over our shoulders. I am learning that people will be who they are with no help or hindrance from me. I heed my sister's words that I need to be intentional with what energy I let in and with what energy I repel. I still occasionally find the dark corners, but I mostly try to keep my eyes looking up, to the mountains and the sky. Every now and again, and even after these many years, though, I still dream of Hertrudes.

Hertrudes went to the beach at Sliding Rock. She went after a storm because that is when it is time to visit the ocean. She sat in a tide pool and brushed at the caressing arms of seaweed on the walls of the pool as it breathed in the moving water. A hawksbill turtle swam up to the outside of the pool. Hertrudes pulled the plumeria flower from where she had tucked it behind her ear and offered it up to the turtle. The sweetness of the flower always made her inexplicably sad and she proffered it in hopes that she would be rid of the cloying melancholy that pervaded her senses. The hawksbill turtle took the blossom in her beak. She looked hard at Hertrudes and slowly blinked before slowly and gracefully extending her flippers and gliding off through open water. Hertrudes watched the hawksbill turtle until she was no longer visible through the deep blue-black sea. She climbed out of the tide pool, shook the water out of her silver hair, and trudged home.

Epilogue—The SOS Hepl Letter

In March 1999, months before our lawsuit was filed, the first group of Vietnamese workers at Daewoosa had been there for almost two months but had yet to be paid. Many had traveled to American Samoa the month before with as little as $20, and now that money had run out. Four of the more outspoken women approached Daewoosa factory owner Lee and asked for their wages. He refused and threatened to punish them.

The situation soon became so dire that a few of the workers decided they must communicate with someone—anyone—on the outside of the compound. They needed help, and soon. Several of the workers wrote a passionate letter pleading for help. They enlisted the highly competent assistance of Ms. Dao Lien, a worker who functioned as the Vietnamese, Korean, and English interpreter for the sweatshop owner.

The workers showed Ms. Lien their letter. Written in Vietnamese, it was a page-long, fastidiously lettered, plaintive appeal for help. Across the top of the page were the letters SOS, written large and dark. Ms. Lien read the letter, approved heartily, and added a PS in broken English: "Hepl us. Please hepl us." Then she hid the letter in her suitcase.

When the obstreperous workers next asked Kil-Soo Lee for their wages, he went into a rage, turned over cafeteria tables, and called the American Samoa police. He had the four women, including one of the workers who had helped write the letter, thrown in the Tafuna Correctional Facility. They were to await deportation back to Vietnam. Forced deportation as a means of labor control—not very original, but astoundingly effective in the territory. Ms. Lien was not among those put in prison.

Since the American Samoa government does not always feed its prisoners in accordance with their particular culinary needs, Lee allowed two of the workers to take food to the imprisoned women at the Tafuna Correctional Facility. One of the workers chosen to go was Ms. Lien. A large Samoan manager and one of the Vietnamese labor bosses accompanied the workers—they were obviously taking no chances. On the way to the prison, Ms. Lien asked the men to stop at a bush store so she could buy milk for the imprisoned women. The men acquiesced but balked when she attempted to get out of the car. They locked her in, laughing, and went into the store for the milk themselves.

Ms. Lien sat in the car and waited. She saw a small man come out of the store and walk across the parking lot to another vehicle. The man looked Vietnamese. Ms. Lien knew that sometimes fishermen on the tuna boats were Vietnamese; at least that was what she had heard. She rolled down her window and extracted the page-long "SOS Hepl" letter from where she had hidden it. She wadded it up into a sweaty little ball, surreptitiously rolled down her window the rest of the way, and tossed it at the Vietnamese man. It bounced off his leg.

The fisherman reached down and picked up the letter. He looked around but did not see Ms. Lien. He continued to his car, smoothing the letter against his leg so he could read it later.

Now it is the criminal trial of Kil-Soo Lee, almost four years later. The "prosecutor angels" Susan Lynn and Robert have spent the past twenty-one months preparing their case, amassing a huge amount of evidence, and preparing the witnesses. They have just brought over their final group of witnesses for the trial—sixteen of the workers among those who had returned to Vietnam. Many were women who had been deported by Kil-Soo Lee in early 1999, those who had been imprisoned in American Samoa. Also in the group was Ms. Dao Lien. Susan Lynn interviewed countless Daewoosa workers in anticipation of the massive criminal trial. Among those she interviewed was Ms. Lien. Susan Lynn listened to her accounts of the conditions at the Daewoosa compound and heard Ms. Lien describe the awful food and cramped barracks. She showed Ms. Lien lots of papers: Daewoosa contracts and management memos and other documents. But when Susan Lynn showed her a crumpled-up page-long letter that said SOS across the top, written large and dark, Ms. Lien folded her head into her arms and wept. It was the letter she had tossed to the Vietnamese man more than four years ago.

Susan Lynn discovered that the Vietnamese man, who was indeed a fisherman, read the letter and took it to the Seafarer's Center in Pago Pago. The Seafarer's Center, a charitable Baptist organization, lent great support and succor to persons who traveled by water. The Vietnamese man gave it to one of the missionaries at the center. The missionary was appalled at the content of the letter and showed it to another missionary. Together they visited the Daewoosa compound but were told to leave by the ASG police or face arrest. The missionary tried to show the letter to the ASG authorities, but they were less than interested. Almost four years later, he gave it to Susan Lynn when she interviewed him, in anticipation of trial.